CROSSCURRENTS
PURSUING SOCIAL JUSTICE AND INTERRELIGIOUS WORK
SINCE 1950

CrossCurrents (ISSN 0011-1953; online ISSN 1939-3881) connects the wisdom of the heart with the life of the mind and the experiences of the body. The journal is operated through its parent organization, the Association for Public Religion and Intellectual Life (APRIL), an interreligious network of academics, activists, artists, and community leaders seeking to engage the many ways religion meets the public. Contributions to the journal exist at the nexus of religion, education, the arts, and social justice. The journal is published quarterly on behalf of the Association for Public Religion and Intellectual Life by the University of North Carolina Press.

The Association for Public Religion and Intellectual Life (formerly ARIL) is a global network of leaders, scholars, and social change agents who explore religious life, engage in intellectual inquiry, and lead ethical action in the world today. Their primary objective, especially through annual summer colloquia and *CrossCurrents*, is to bring together leading voices of our time to advocate for justice and to examine global spiritual and interreligious currents in both historical and contemporary perspectives.

A membership to APRIL includes access to *CrossCurrents* starting with Volume 58, 2008, though our partners at Project MUSE, monthly newsletters, early access to summer colloquium themes, a 40% on UNC Press books, and more. For more information, including membership and subscription rates, visit www.aprilonline.org.

This reissue of *CrossCurrents* was one of four issues published in 2019 as part of Volume 69. For a current masthead visit www.aprilonline.org.

© 2019 Association for Public Religion and Intellectual Life. All rights reserved.

ISBN 978-1-4696-6709-6 (Print)

CROSS CURRENTS

RELIGION AND SEX / UALITIES
Edited by Samuel B. Davis and Pamela D. Winfield

347
Introduction
Samuel B. Davis and Pamela D. Winfield

351
Erastes-Eromenos Relationships in Two Ancient Epics
Morgan van Kesteren

365
Rumi: The Homoerotic Sufi Saint
Delaney James

384
Leah and Hagar: An Intergenerational Conversation of Belonging
Ashley Starr-Morris

402
Queer Nuns and Genderbending Saints: Genderf*cking Notions of Normativity
Jessi Knippel

415
Need We Still Ask Why? Theodical Futurism and the Sinthomosexual God
Samuel B. Davis

439
The First #MeToo Activists: Contemporary Campaigning in Support of the Former Japanese Military "Comfort Women"
Caroline Norma

462
Interview with Dr. Robert Orsi (Northwestern University)
Samuel B. Davis and Pamela D. Winfield

468
Best of Brothers, Finest of Men, Or …?
Peter Heinegg

473
Notes on Contributors

About the Cover: Cover photo used with permission iStock Photos and bikeworldtravel.

CROSSCURRENTS
INTRODUCTION

When *CrossCurrents* invited me to co-edit a journal issue around the theme of "sex and religion," my excitement could scarcely be contained. As a scholar whose work lies squarely at the intersection of religious studies and human sexuality, it has been both professionally and personally fulfilling for me to compile and publish new young voices in the field, complemented by a special interview with leading scholar of American Catholicism, Dr. Robert Orsi.

I initially organized a graduate symposium on this topic at the University of North Carolina—Charlotte in the Spring of 2019, and we gathered additional scholars to fill out the issue. When initially discussing the theme for the conference that this journal is based on, some expressed concern that the specific topic of "sex," especially as it relates to "religion," was not broad enough. However, as the articles in this issue rightly show, there is a wide range of possible projects. Furthermore, they all take up what the late J.Z. Smith identifies as the most important question for the academy to ask: "So what?"[1] The articles here all address this question, either explicitly or implicitly, mostly perhaps because it is nigh impossible to avoid in this context. Whether discussing the significance of overlooked figures in biblical literature, challenging harmful pervasive cultural norms, or bringing attention to the historical significance of certain sexual acts, the importance of each inquiry is undeniable.

As Kathryn Lofton, Professor of Religious Studies at Yale University, notes that when discussing the terms "religion" and "sexuality," "any definition of the one will lead to the other: the history of sexuality and the history of religion are co-constitutive."[2] Eventually, discussing either religion or sex/sexuality will inevitably lead to discussing some aspect of the other. Likewise, our esteemed contributing scholar, Dr. Robert Orsi, aptly states in his interview,

> It's time that we put sexuality fully into the study of the history of Catholicism (as Foucault, who grew up Catholic, would agree). And

> I don't mean in the sense of prohibitions, but of the dynamic between prohibition and permission, of the interplay of denial and desire and what comes of it.

I agree fully with Dr. Orsi's assertion, but I would expand the purview to say that it is indeed time to put sexuality fully into the study of religion in general, not just the history of Catholicism. Again, not simply in the sense of prohibitions, but as a reality, something that does not and cannot exist or be examined in isolation. We therefore asked our writers to contribute as broadly as possible within the framework we provided, and they delivered.

Morgan van Kesteren of Colgate University offers up an in-depth look at two widely known Greek epics, Virgil's *Aeneid* and Homer's *Iliad*, specifically identifying places in the text that highlight ancient Greek societal and theoretical understandings of male homosexual relations. She guides us through what she identifies as the erastes-eromenos intimacies of Nisus and Euryalus and of Achilles and Patroclus, given as analogous examples of heavenly love as understood by Plato. On the other hand, van Kesteren argues that the relationships between Dido and Aeneas and Paris and Helen, again through Plato, are better understood as examples of common love. She goes on to say that within ancient Greek society, the heavenly love relationships found between the men in these stories would have been regarded as a "sacred exchange of wisdom and protection," and thus far more societally beneficial than the seemingly hindering and even destructive heterosexual relationships.

Delany James takes up the question of the existence of homoeroticism within the poetry of Rumi, the popularized thirteenth-century Sufi poet. James dissects the writings of Rumi, identifying the places that show an intense love and longing for his teacher, Shams-Tabrizi, the person to whom all Rumi's writings are dedicated. Placing it within the context of cultural attitudes toward sexual and homosexual behavior in medieval Turkey, James argues that Rumi's poetry can best be understood as homoerotic, directed toward his teacher and master Shams-Tabrizi.

Ashley Starr-Morris picks up on a striking similarity between the biblical narratives of Leah and Hagar, positioning them in relation to their matriarch counterparts, Sarah and Rachel. Reminding us that repetition in the Hebrew Bible should always give pause, Starr-Morris argues that by looking at the stories of Leah and Hagar intergenerationally, they lend each other a significance that wouldn't be as visible when read separately. She shows us that, although regularly cast aside by their wife counterparts or the men themselves, Leah and Hagar are undeniably vital in the long lines of descendants of Israel.

Jessica Knippel from Claremont University investigates the ethnographic work of Dr. Melissa Wilcox on the Sisters of Perpetual Indulgence, an intentionally parodic queer activist group that embodies certain aspects of Catholic sisterhood. She attempts the daring task of placing what she describes as a "cross between RuPaul's Drag Race and traditional Catholic habits" within a larger legacy of gender-bending sainthood within the Catholic tradition. Juxtaposing the modern Sisters with saints Marinus, Pelagia, Perpetua, and Wilgefortis, each of whom blurred gender lines, Knippel argues that both present performative creations of self-agency.

In my own essay, I look to the Hebrew book of Job as a source worth investigating in queer studies, not just for its intriguingly unique style, but as a boundary-pushing narrative that actually challenges a more traditional reading as a theodicy. Utilizing Lee Edelman's *No Future: Queer Theory and the Death Drive* as a theoretical framework, I argue that Job's God embodies what Edelman calls the "sinthomosexual," a figure defined by its defiance of social norms. I further argue that the value of the Book of Job lies in pointing out just how harmful it is to judge and vilify based on the presumption of wrongdoing, as Jerry Falwell did when blaming the 9/11 attacks on "gays" and "abortionists" and saying "God will not be mocked," or as Pastor John Hagee did, saying that hurricane Katrina was God punishing New Orleans for scheduling a gay pride parade.

Caroline Norman from the University of Melbourne, Australia, explores a different, more ethically oriented tack as she discusses the military sexual slavery of so-called "comfort women" during World War II. Her article provides a historically informed ethical argument that holds repercussions for the larger sex industry throughout Northeast Asia today.

Finally, our interview with Dr. Robert Orsi provides an enticing introduction to his forthcoming book on Catholic sexual abuse, entitled *Give Us Boys*. Drawing on unprecedented access to first-hand survivor accounts and archival research, this ethnographic and historical study demonstrates how "the Catholic closet made sexuality horribly dangerous for women, for children, for the vulnerable, even as it put into place immense institutions to care for the victims it helped create." Most disturbingly, he argues that "It's not a 'crisis'. It's the modern Catholic normal," and critiques the "willful naïveté" of Catholics who think it has been adequately addressed internally. For him as well as for all the contributors to this volume, therefore, "sexuality is not peripheral to the study of religion, but integral to it."

Notes

1. Jonathan Z. Smith and Christopher I. Lehrich, *On Teaching Religion : Essays by Jonathan Z. Smith* (New York: Oxford University Press, 2013), 58.
2. Kent Brintnall, *Religion : Embodied Religion*, Macmillan Interdisciplinary Handbooks (Farmington Hills, Mich: Macmillan Reference USA, a part of Gale, Cengage Learning, 2016), 19.

—Samuel B. Davis and Pamela D. Winfield

CROSSCURRENTS
ERASTES-EROMENOS RELATIONSHIPS IN TWO ANCIENT EPICS

Morgan van Kesteren

When reading ancient epics, such as Virgil's *Aeneid* (Pharr 1964; West 1990) and Homer's *Iliad*, parallels can be discerned from the complexities that lie underneath relations between certain characters, which highlight cultural aspects of ancient society. There exist undeniable similarities between the examples of heavenly love, Nisus and Euryalus from the *Aeneid* and Achilles and Patroclus from the *Iliad*, and the examples of common love, Dido and Aeneas from the *Aeneid* and Paris and Helen from the *Iliad*. Plato's *Symposium* provides further insight into how ancient philosophers considered homosexual relations and what they deemed beneficial out of the love that two people share. In short, this paper argues that Plato's *Symposium* can help provide insight into Virgil's and Homer's attitudes toward spiritual love and a more sexual love. This paper is organized into two main sections, focusing on the respective characters from the *Aeneid* and the *Iliad*. Each section provides a brief summary of the events of that epic, followed by examples from each story placed within the theoretical context of Plato's explorations of love in the *Symposium*. Through close reading of these texts, this paper provides the reader with a sense of how homosexual relations have been understood and portrayed through the works of Virgil, Homer, and Plato.

The Aeneid
In his epic, Virgil whisks the reader through the Trojan warrior Aeneas' journey as he, among the other Trojans, is forced to leave their land,

defeated by the Greeks in the Trojan War, and eventually found Rome. The obstacles that Aeneas and his men face are the workings of the goddess Juno, who resents the Trojans and tries to prevent them from reaching the shores of Italy, even though Aeneas is destined to found Rome. Along their journey, a storm incited by Juno's envious rage drowns many of his men, but Neptune guides Aeneas and the rest of the Trojan warriors safely to the shores of Carthage. Aeneas's mother, the goddess Venus, empathizes with her distressed son and resolves to make his stay in Carthage pleasurable by providing Aeneas with the company of a lover. Under Venus's command, Cupid strikes Dido, Queen of Carthage, with his arrow, causing Dido to fall head over heels for Aeneas. Lovesick Dido is quickly disappointed when her lover Aeneas must abandon her to continue his journey and fulfill his destiny, as determined by Jupiter. Devastated by Aeneas's betrayal, Dido believes the only way to ease her pain is to commit suicide. This tragic love story of Dido and Aeneas reminds the reader that many of Virgil's characters are simply pawns of the gods and only serve to promote the founding of Rome.

While reading the *Aeneid*, certain relations between characters, like Nisus and Euryalus and Aeneas and Pallas, resonate as examples of the heavenly love depicted in Plato's *Symposium*. Plato's *Symposium* exposes various ancient Greek philosophers' understandings about the goddess of Love, and it exposes the different motivations behind each type of love. Phaedrus, one of the ancient Greek philosophers, suggests that love between an older man and a younger man is most effective in guiding men to lead good lives, more so than the family, the state, or money, because this love teaches men shame when behaving disgracefully. Pausanias, another ancient Greek philosopher, strengthens Phaedrus' theory by describing two different goddesses of love, Heavenly Aphrodite and Common Aphrodite, and associating them with two different types of love, heavenly love and common love. According to Pausanias, common love is deemed bad because it consists of attraction only between the bodies of a man and a woman and not between minds. Heavenly love, on the other hand, is only shared between two males and consists of a loved one who gratifies his lover, or his mentor, in exchange for wisdom and gaining virtue. When recognizing Pausanias' two different types of love in the *Aeneid*, we observe that common love, like the love between Dido and

5.334-335). As Euryalus finds himself victorious in the foot race, Virgil exploits "his beauty as he stood there weeping and the manly spirit growing in that lovely body" (Virgil 2.344-345).[5] The descriptions of both Nisus and Euryalus after the foot race impeccably align with their initial characterizations: Nisus demonstrates his devotion to his beloved by ensuring Euryalus' victory, for he considers a victory for one of them as a victory for both of them, and Virgil again chooses to focus on capturing Euryalus' beauty and pride when victorious. Virgil's initial description of the two Trojan lovers and the events that take place in the foot race expose Nisus's and Euryalus's weaknesses and foreshadow their transgressions during their mission in Book 6, which inevitably submit them to their deaths.

Examining Plato's *Symposium* to contrast the love between Nisus and Euryalus and Dido and Aeneas provides an understanding to societal connotations of love, and how the *Aeneid* is charged with relationships of heavenly love and common love. In the *Symposium*, Pausanias expresses that heavenly love is only directed toward males, whereas common love typically describes the love between a man and a woman because it is based solely on physical attraction and is therefore less pure. The understanding of these two different types of love compliments the love between Dido and Aeneas, which for Aeneas was likely just a sexual relationship and the deeper love of Nisus and Euryalus. Pausanias explains that common lovers "are attracted to...bodies rather than minds," reminding the reader of the "cave scene" in Book 4 and the uncertainty of what actually took place in the cave: marriage or was it simply sex.[6] The notion that Dido and Aeneas' love is common questions the extent of how romanticized their love is and if their relationship is strictly physical, especially compared to the heavenly love of Nisus and Euryalus. One of the few moments Virgil presents the reader with the unity of Dido and Aeneas and alludes to any sort of marriage between them is his description of Aeneas through Mercury's eyes after the events that took place in the cave: "His sword was studded with yellow stars of jasper, and glowing with Tyrian purple there hung from his shoulders a rich cloak given him by Dido into which she had woven a fine cross-thread of gold" (Virgil 4.261-264).[7] Aeneas is depicted as wearing Carthaginian dress, conforming to Carthaginian society, which denotes a unification of Aeneas and Dido and Aeneas and the entire city of Carthage. His cloak of purple and gold remind the reader of Dido's cloak that she wore on the hunt, right before their marriage in the cave, and the fact that the cloak is described as in the Latin as "ardebat" alludes to the burning passion of Aeneas and Dido's love. "Ardebat" is commonly translated as "was burning" or "was in love." This translation symbolizes the cloak as a token of Dido's affection for Aeneas. In addition, Dido is subtly portrayed as a traditional, domestic wife by forging Aeneas's clothes for him, further suggesting a true marriage between them. This imagery, however, does not allude to the same kind of passionate love as the imagery of Nisus and Euryalus' intimate deaths. The intertwinement of Nisus and Euryalus establishes the deep bond between themselves and their souls as they vanish together, whereas the description of the traditional marriage between Aeneas and Dido emphasizes prosperity from this political union and their legacy from family and procreation.

Another moment where Dido and Aeneas' love is described as consuming both of them is "how they were even now indulging themselves and keeping each other warm the whole winter through, forgetting about their kingdoms and becoming the slaves of lust."[8] Virgil's description of Aeneas and Dido as both "neglecting their duties" and as both "becoming the slaves of lust" denotes that Aeneas too was at one point infatuated with desire for Dido, but he is portrayed here as showing interest strictly in their physical relationship, especially with the Latin "fovere," or to keep warm or to cherish, as a sexually charged word. This willy-nilly behavior of forgetting responsibilities caused by desire for one another is similar to the reckless behavior of Nisus and Euryalus when they savagely slay Rutulians, perhaps to not only prove their worth to their leader Aeneas and the other Trojans warriors, but also to impress each other. This connects to Phaedrus' description of love and how love guides men to lead good lives. He expresses that love leads men to be more conscious of their behavior, concerned with what their loved one will think: "Take the case of a man in love who is caught acting disgracefully or undergoing something disgraceful because he fails to defend himself out of cowardice. I think it would cause him more pain to be seen in this situation by his boyfriend than by his father, his friends or anyone else."[9] This concept of two men who love each other and therefore want to do everything right in each other's eyes epitomizes the love of Nisus and Euryalus and provides a reasoning behind the extent of their killings. Phaedrus claims that an army of lovers would be the most successful army: "Theirs would be the best possible system of society, for they would hold back from all that is shameful, and seek honor in each other's eyes."[10] Following Phaedrus's theories on love, the multitude of Nisus's and Euryalus's killings is likely a display of their bravery, motivated by the urge to be their best selves in front of their lover.

The love between Nisus and Euryalus is emphasized by their shared love for glory, plunder, and battle.[11] Expressing similar interests and goals intensifies the bond between the two warriors and makes their love eternal, unlike Dido and Aeneas. Scholar Lee Fratantuono claims, "Nisus and Euryalus die together and in love, and so in death, perversely, they constitute the only 'successful' couple in the epic."[12] Aside from their shared goals as warriors, Nisus and Euryalus expose differences in their demeanor during their expedition to retrieve Aeneas. As they slay the sleeping Rutulians, they are both compared to animals slaughtering their prey; however, Euryalus is described as less in control then Nisus, for he was "in a blazing frenzy."[13] When Nisus "noticed Euryalus was being carried away by bloodlust and greed,"[14] he tries to warn his loved one and convince him to continue on with their mission, relating to Pausanias' idea of the erastes-eromenos relationship.[15] The romantic relationship between the elder Nisus and the younger Euryalus is embodied by the erastes-eromenos relationship, which Pausanias claims to be heavenly love and appropriate under these circumstances: "when lover and boyfriend come together, each observing the appropriate rule: that the lover is justified in any service he performs for the boyfriend who gratifies him, and that the boyfriend is justified in any favour he does for someone who is making him wise and good. Also, the lover must be able to develop the boyfriend's understanding and virtue in general, and the boyfriend must want to acquire education and wisdom in general."[16] This heavenly love, in which the younger is supposed to learn from the elder, is expressed as Nisus voices concern for Euryalus's savage behavior and urges him to follow Nisus's lead by continuing with the mission. The unspoken agreement of an erastes-eromenos relationship establishes a much stronger connection between the two lovers because they are connected to each other both mentally and physically, as opposed to the physical love between Dido and Aeneas.

Similar to Nisus and Euryalus' love, yet less apparent, is the relationship between Aeneas and Pallas which can also be understood as eroticized and another example of erastes-eromenos. Virgil explicitly describes their relationship as a mentoring one with Evander's words "Let him be hardened to the rigours of war under your leadership. Let him daily see your conduct and admire you from his earliest years correlating to the loved taught virtues and wisdom by the lover."[17] More apparent is the familial relationship between the two with a father teaching a young boy and guiding him so that he may follow in his footsteps. However, there are subtle sexual innuendos that point to the possibility of a more sexual relationship like erastes-eromenos between Aeneas and Pallas. When Aeneas and Pallas first embrace, "he (Pallas) took Aeneas by the right hand in a long clasp" (Virgil 8.124-125).[18] Scholar Michael Putnam claims, "the line heaps chiasmus on chiasmus to convey, through sound and verbal deployment, the intensity of Pallas' gesture."[19] The use of the words "long" and "clasp" provides the reader with a sense of eternity and unity between the two, demonstrating their devotion to this friendship or erastes-eromenos partnership. The use of "right hand" denotes further a romantic relationship, for "right hand" can have the connotation of marriage and is used in Book 4 by Dido herself as she questions her fleeing lover: "Did you think you could slip away from this land of mine and say nothing? Does our love have no claim on you? Or the pledge your right hand once gave me?"[20] In a similar manner of Nisus consumed only with the thought of avenging his lover as Euryalus dies, Aeneas recognizes Pallas' armor on Turnus, motivating him to drive his sword through Turnus. After remembering his beloved Pallas, Aeneas is described as "burning with mad passion and terrible in his wrath"[21] and "blazing with rage" (Virgil 12.950),[22] alluding to the deep passion Aeneas feels for his eromenos and his urge to avenge the Pallas he cherished.[23]

Presenting the reader with underlying themes of common love and heavenly love, Virgil possibly exploits his own opinions about love and how the kind of love one would die for is the love that establishes a deep connection between the minds of two men. Familial love, though less romantic and erotic, is another version of love that is carried out throughout the *Aeneid*, and one that should not be overlooked. The love that Aeneas has for Anchises, his father, and Ascanius, his son, surpasses the love he has for his Trojan wife Creusa, for he chooses to carry his mentor and the one he mentors, leaving Creusa to die with burning Troy. Familial love like Pausanias' heavenly love is based on the sharing of wisdom between two people and the idea of passing on the torch, as opposed to love based simply on sexual desire. Looking at their relationship from Dido's perspective, however, she would say that there were real feelings and a deep connection between her and Aeneas. This possible misconception, based on the actions of Aeneas, sparked her suicide, proving the disorderly nature of common love. Simply attributing love in the *Aeneid* to only the love story of Dido and Aeneas does not account for the various types of love depicted in the *Aeneid*, and this notion removes the examination of other intimate relationships that drive the actions of certain characters.

The Iliad

The *Aeneid* is not the only ancient epic where different types of love seep through the pages. Exempla of common love and heavenly love are also embedded in Homer's *Iliad*, with the common love between Paris and Helen and the heavenly love between warriors Achilles and Patroclus. As Virgil found inspiration through Homer's epics, the similarities between the erastes-eromenos relationships of Trojan warriors Nisus and Euryalus and Achaean warriors Achilles and Pallas are uncanny. The *Iliad* takes place nine years after the start of the Trojan War, a war between the Trojans and the Achaeans, incited by Trojan Prince Paris's "capture" of Helen, Queen of Sparta. The story opens with the Achaeans capturing two beautiful Trojan maidens as prisoners of war. King Agamemnon presented one of the maidens as a gift to his cherished warrior Achilles and kept the other maiden for himself. However, because one of the maiden's fathers was a priest for Apollo, Apollo rained a thousand arrows down on the Achaeans, killing much of Agamemnon's army. With many of his men dead, Agamemnon surrendered his prisoner of war and takes Achilles's for himself to replace this loss. Furious with Agamemnon for stealing his prize, Achilles refuses to fight for his king. In the absence of the mighty warrior Achilles from the battlefield, the Achaeans suffer many losses and nearly get destroyed by the Trojans. Proud Achilles finally agrees to contribute to the war efforts of the Achaeans by allowing his beloved Patroclus fight in his place, even wearing his own armor. Patroclus, embodying the strength of Achilles, excels in battle and for a short time the Achaeans triumph in the Trojan War. When Trojan Hector slays Patroclus, Achilles is stunned and filled with rage and sets out to avenge his beloved. Achilles ferociously decimates Hector taunting the Trojans by dragging the corpse behind his chariot, emphasizing the deep connection and love he feels toward Patroclus, fearlessly avenging him.

An epic seemingly based on the events of the Trojan War, filled with battle, plunder, blood, and glory, the *Iliad* exposes the love involved in the relations between certain warriors. With the memorable example of common love embodied in the relationship between Paris and Helen, and the erastes-eromenos relationship between the Achaean warriors Achilles and Patroclus, the *Iliad* exposes more about ancient Greek customs than simply war tactics and battle history. Even though there is less romantic imagery surrounding Achilles and Patroclus, compared to Nisus and Euryalus in the *Aeneid*, the description of Achilles's reaction to the death of Patroclus resembles that of a mother mourning the loss of her child. The disheveled description of Achilles, broken by the news of his beloved, reveals the vast depths of the love and care intertwining Achilles and Patroclus.

The ambiguity behind the so-called "capture" of Helen parallels the ambiguity associated with the so-called "marriage" of Dido and Aeneas. Helen may have willingly gone with Paris to Troy, escaping her duties as Queen of Sparta to enjoy the luxuries of Troy and indulge in the lust between her and the handsome Paris. In both cases, the pairs of lovers were swept away by their lust for one another, neglecting their duties and their roles in promoting society. Whether Paris selfishly seized Helen as his prize or Helen stole away in the night with her secret lover, this sexual attraction and infatuation between them made them blind to their societal obligations. Similarly, the physical connection between Dido and Aeneas causes both of them to neglect their duties and forget their purpose. The Greek philosophers of Plato's *Symposium* consider this type of love or sexual desire as toxic, hindering society's progress. Both the common love between Paris and Helen and Dido and Aeneas led to complete destruction of a civilization: For the fleeing of Paris and Helen incited the Trojan War and contributed to the downfall of Troy and the irresponsibility that went hand in hand with the physical love between Dido and Aeneas led to the downfall of Carthage and decelerated the founding of Rome. Compared to heavenly love that emphasizes the exchange of wisdom and perhaps certain political or social favors, both Virgil and Homer demonstrate how this common love is too distracting and serves as a weakness. Common love as weakness is exploited by the gods throughout epic, as they intervene with human affairs by introducing temptations to further the agenda of one god as they compete with another. For example, Venus, the mother of Aeneas, has Cupid strike Dido with his arrow to make Aeneas' stay more pleasurable in Carthage, since Juno delayed his journey to Rome by calling on the god of the winds to blow Aeneas and his men off course. Venus' intervention in Aeneas' affairs by providing him with a lover ignites this common love between Aeneas and Dido, distracting him from his mission with temptation, as she wants her son to indulge in the pleasures of life and forget about his hardships.

Through the death of Patroclus, the erastes-eromenos relationship between Achilles and Patroclus becomes apparent, with the intensity of Achilles' grief for his lost beloved and the extent to which Achilles feels compelled to avenge his beloved. With the Achaeans struggling in battle, Achilles, who excused himself from fighting with the Achaeans to spite Agamemnon, finally agrees to assist the Achaean army by allowing his companion Patroclus to fight. Patroclus, dressed in the mighty warrior Achilles' armor, instills hope among the Achaean army. This hope is soon squandered, however, when Achilles' armor is stripped from him, revealing his identity as Patroclus, and as Hector executes him in the battlefield. When news of his beloved Patroclus' death reaches Achilles, Achilles is stunned with grief and rage: "A black cloud of grief came shrouding over Achilles. Both hands clawing the ground for soot and filth, he poured it over his head, fouled his handsome face and black ashes settled onto his fresh clean war-shirt. Overpowered in all his power, sprawled in the dust, Achilles lay there, fallen... tearing his hair, defiling it with his own hands."[24] This "black cloud of grief" and Homer's depiction of Achilles as so distraught that he covers himself in dirt and pulls out his hair allude to the deep erastes-eromenos relationship between Achilles and Patroclus and how crazed Achilles feels with this loss. Achilles beats the ground as someone who is truly devastated by the loss of a loved one, to the point where they may blame themselves and feel as though they cannot move on. Achilles was so distraught by the news of the death of his beloved Patroclus that he burst out "Then let me die at once."25 Similar to Nisus' reaction of wanting nothing but revenge, Achilles seeks out to destroy Hector, knowing that he is likely submitting himself to his own death in doing so. By willingly sacrificing themselves to join their lovers in the afterlife, Nisus and Achilles epitomize these soldiers intertwined with their eromenos, further emphasizing the sanction behind an army of lovers.

Besides the self-sacrificing nature of the erastes-eromenos relationship between Achilles and Patroclus, the mentorship and true sharing of wisdom nature of the erastes-eromenos relationship is exposed. When Achilles allows Patroclus to fight in his place and even wear his armor, he provides him with instructions to only fight long enough to save the burning Achaean ships. Just the fact that Achilles allows his beloved Patroclus to take his place in battle and basically pretend to be him speaks much to the love that Achilles feels toward Patroclus. Achilles is a proud warrior, as exposed earlier in the epic when he sulks over Agamemnon taking away his prisoner of war. Giving Patroclus the opportunity to embody Achilles and succeed in battle for them both demonstrates that even though Achilles is proud, this pride encompasses his beloved Patroclus. Similar to how Nisus and Euryalus share in their search for glory when they slay the Rutilians, Achilles and Patroclus almost become one, as Patroclus is given the opportunity to make his erastes proud and live up to Achilles' legacy on the battlefield. Interestingly, demonstrating the mentoring aspect of the relationship between Achilles and Patroclus, Homer explicitly states that it was not until after Patroclus wore Achilles' armor did the fate of the Achaeans in battle turn in their favor. Both Nisus and Achilles warn their loved ones and give them specific orders to ensure their safety. While Nisus advises Euryalus not to get carried away in his slayings of the Rutilians, Achilles warns Patroclus to contribute only to the efforts of the war until the Achaeans stopped the Trojans from burning their ships, so he does not find himself in danger with Hector. As the older, wiser soldiers in their erastes-eromenos relationships, Nisus and Achilles mentor their lovers and are deeply concerned with their well-being, rightfully so, as Euryalus and Patroclus, so motivated by killings disobey their erastes. Both Euryalus and Patroclus cannot control themselves while slaying their enemies, flooded with this desire to cut down every enemy that steps in their paths. This flawed trait of both younger soldiers, fueled by their desire for glory in battle, inevitable leads them to their downfall.

Conclusion

Throughout both epics the *Aeneid* and the *Iliad*, the examples of common love with Dido and Aeneas and Paris and Helen prove to be the most destructive in the progression of ancient civilization. When Dido and Aeneas are infatuated with one another, all construction of buildings in Carthage seize, slowing down the progression of Carthaginian society, as Dido neglects her duties as queen. With the fleeing of Paris and Helen resulting in the Trojan War, countless men on both sides die in battle and the city of Troy crumbles. Even though the erastes-eromenos relationships between Nisus and Euryalus and Achilles and Patroclus seem to be flawed or fail, as both Euryalus and Patroclus are killed, resulting in the deaths of Nisus and Achilles, these relationships do not directly result in the destruction of a city or the death of thousands. These examples of heavenly love do not directly affect the survival of populations or the advancements of civilizations, but rather they only seemingly impact the two parties involved, the erastes and the eromenos. Thus, heavenly love between two men and this sacred exchange of wisdom and protection, as explained by Phaedrus and Pausanias, prove to be most beneficial for the progressions of society and hence, divinely protected.

Notes

1. Virgil 9.426-427.
2. Virgil 9.435-438.
3. Virgil 9.446-448.
4. Virgil 5.294-296.
5. Virgil 2.344-345.
6. Plato, and Christopher Gill. The Symposium. London, England: Penguin Books, 1999: 13. Print. Penguin Classics.
7. Virgil 4.261-264.
8. Virgil 4.193-196.
9. Plato, and Christopher Gill. The Symposium. London, England: Penguin Books, 1999: 10. Print. Penguin Classics.
10. Ibid.
11. Fratantuono, Lee. ""Pius Amor": Nisus, Euryalus, and the Footrace of "Aeneid" V." Latomus 69.1 (2010): 51-52. Print.
12. Ibid.

13. Virgil 9.345.
14. Virgil 9.355-356.
15. Ibid.
16. Plato, and Christopher Gill. The Symposium. London, England: Penguin Books, 1999: 17. Print. Penguin Classics.
17. Virgil 8.516-518.
18. Virgil 8.124-125.
19. Putnam, Michael C. J. *Virgil's Aeneid: Interpretation and Influence*. Chapel Hill: University of North Carolina Press, 1995: 33. Print.
20. Virgil 4.307-309v.
21. Virgil 12.945-946.
22. Virgil 12.950.
23. Ibid.
24. Homer 18.24-30.
25. Homer 18.114.

Works Cited

Fratantuono, Lee, 2010, ""Pius Amor": Nisus, Euryalus, and the Footrace of "Aeneid" V," Latomus **69**(1): 43–55.

Pharr, Clyde, 1964, Vergil's Aeneid Books I-IV: Revised Edition, Lexington, MA: DC Heath and Company.

Plato, Christopher Gill, 1999, The Symposium (Penguin Classics), London, UK: Penguin Books.

Putnam, Michael C. J., 1995, Virgil's Aeneid: Interpretation and Influence, Chapel Hill, NC: University of North Carolina Press.

West David, 1990, "Virgil: The Aeneid," A New Prose Translation: 114. Print.

CROSSCURRENTS

RUMI
The Homoerotic Sufi Saint

Delaney James

Expressions of sexuality, specifically homoerotic poetry, in mystical writings are by no means uncommon. Wendy Noel DeSouza examines Louis Massignon's explicit expressions of homosexuality through his translations of Sufi mystical love writings.[1] Paul Losensky documents the commonality of homosexual tendencies in the Persian poet Muhtasham's works, specifically *The Lover's Confection*.[2] Amira El-Zein writes that Rumi's encounter with Shams-Tabrizi sparked Rumi's poetic nature and notes that all his poetry is addressed to him.[3]

With El-Zein's background on Rumi's life (1207–1273) in consideration, this article will analyze Rumi's love poetry dedicated to his teacher Shams-Tabrizi (1185–1248). Specifically, it will first introduce Rumi's itinerant life and his discipleship under Shams. It will then contextualize Rumi's poetry within the conventional sexual norms of the eastern Mediterranean (present-day Turkey), where long-standing Hellenistic ideals of male-male relations coexisted alongside the cultural norms of premodern Islam. It will finally examine the explicitly sexual imagery within Rumi's poetry, noting the crude imagery of selected passages versus the overtly loving imagery found in the many devotional verses dedicated to his spiritual guide.

Such analysis is important for several reasons. While homoeroticism in Rumi's poetry has not gone unnoticed by scholars in the field, such as Mahdi Tourage and Ali A. El-Huni, this work will firstly contribute to the literature by contextualizing Rumi's poetry to his spiritual guide Shams-Tabrizi within the much larger cultural milieu of Greco-Roman and

Islamic culture in the Eastern Mediterranean. Secondly, it queers previous assumptions about the marriage/lover trope in mysticism studies, which Evelyn Underhill most clearly articulated by assuming and asserting that the "Spiritual Marriage" is a heteronormative one.[4] Finally and by extension, this study redefines the nature of erotic mystical poetry in general. Usually, erotic verses dedicated to the Divine are understood to be a metaphor for the poet's longing for intimacy with their God. In Islam, Allah is neither male nor female; but in Rumi's love poetry, the subject he longs for takes on a distinctively male character, which he explicitly imagines as his guide Shams-Tabrizi.

Rumi's life & learning

Rumi's life

Many people today recognize the name Rumi even if they do not have a full understanding of who he was or his contribution to the mystical writings of Islam. Rumi, birth name Jalaluddin Muhammad, was born in 1207. One source claims that he was born in Balkh, Persia, or modern-day Afghanistan, while another cites his birthplace as Vakhsh, Iran.[5] According to El-Zein, Balkh was invaded by Tartars, forcing Jalaluddin and his family to flee to Rum, Konia, or modern-day Turkey.[6] The region Rum is the reason Jalaluddin acquired the name "al-Rumi," or Rumi.[7] However, Lewis writes that Rumi's family left Vakhsh because his father Bahâ al-Din was "denied the rank and prestige he sought."[8] Despite the discrepancies in Rumi's birthplace, both authors agree that the poet migrated to Konia, present-day Turkey. Rumi received a traditional religious studies-education in Aleppo and Damascus, including the study of Hanafi law, Koran, Hadith, and theology.[9] While obtaining this education, Rumi was "initiated into the Sufi path."[10] Once he returned to Konia, he became a recognized and beloved expert in Islamic law, also known as a *mufti*.[11]

People today often recognize Rumi for his poetry; but before Rumi met Shams-Tabrizi, he had never written a single documented verse. Their encounter on November 29, 1244, made "poetry flow from him."[12] "He [Rumi] became more ecstatic in his worship, expressing his love for God not only in a careful attitude of self-renunciation and control, but also through the joy of poetry, music and meditative dance."[13] Shams-

Tabrizi, Rumi's spiritual guide, transformed Rumi's life upon their first meeting and each day thereafter.

The master-disciple relationship

The teacher-student relationship is extremely important within the Islamic sect of Sufism. The goal of a Sufi mystical experience is to "merge with Allah in ecstatic union," or *fana*.[14] Union can only be achieved with the help of a master who is in Allah's favor. The disciple follows the way, or *tariqa*, which is a strict process that will prepare the disciple for their mystical experience.[15]

Unifying experiences such as these occur through religions across the world. Evelyn Underhill describes this type of mystical experience in Christianity as a "Spiritual Marriage" between the Word of God or God Himself and the soul; the Divine is the Bridegroom, and the soul is the Bride.[16] The way in which Underhill describes this mystical experience is heteronormative, assigning the soul the role of "bride." Rumi and Shams' master-disciple relationship, and the poetry it inspired, challenge the heteronormative thinking surrounding mystical-lover experiences with the divine.

According to his autobiography *Me & Rumi*, Shams writes of an eagerness to teach even before meeting Rumi. "I want someone who knows nothing. I want to teach," he writes. [17]Shams also writes, however, that he does not want to teach simply anyone; "I've put my finger on the pulse of those who guide the world to the Real."[18] As a result, through a series of veiled parables, poetry, and writings akin to journal entries, Shams effectively intimates that he considers his student to be God's saint.[19]

Aflaki and Sipehsalar, biographers of Rumi's life, report that Shams and Rumi stayed alone together for a period of approximately six months.[20] During their time together, Rumi learned the *tariqa* from his spiritual guide. Shams vanished after this brief period of time but remained a constant presence throughout the remainder of al-Rumi's life.

Rumors circulated about what came of Shams after he left Rumi. Some say that Rumi's youngest son killed him, another theory is that Shams was killed because of "religious blasphemy," and yet another conjecture states that Shams left Rumi in the night to "become the wandering, wild bird that he was,"[21] that is, to continue the *tariqa* on his own in order to achieve *fana*. Shiva claims that Rumi refused to believe any of these rumors for forty days; after that, Rumi concluded Shams was dead and dressed fully in black from then on to outwardly express his grief.[22] In losing Shams, Rumi not only lost his spiritual master, but he lost what he considered to be the earthly embodiment of God.

Contexts
Homosexuality in the Hellenized Eastern Mediterranean

Many scholars who focus on sexual acts in a different culture and a different period than the ones in which they are writing are careful to not assign sexual identities to the people they study. Mazo Karras outlines the two prevailing schools of thought: essentialism and social constructionism. Essentialism argues that within each culture are people of different sexual orientations; it further argues that sexual orientation is biological and is not chosen.[23] Social constructionism has two camps; one argues that scholars cannot assume sexual identities based on their sexual acts, while the other holds that sexual identities were irrelevant until nineteenth-century Westerners created the concept.[24] This article will adhere in part to essentialism and in part to the first camp of social constructionism. This work will hold to the belief that modern-day readers cannot know the sexual identities of the people it aims to understand as those individuals did not have the words to self-describe their orientation; but it acknowledges that queer people existed throughout history whether or not the word to describe them had yet been invented.

To understand homosexual activity in the Hellenized Middle East better, an explanation of sexual constructs in the Greek Empire is necessary. The Greek Empire fell in 146 BCE to the Romans, but the cultural influence of Greco-Roman civilization persisted throughout the former empire even as successive waves of Christian and Islamic forces took hold. [25]This was especially the case in the eastern Mediterranean, including modern-day Turkey where Rumi spent most of his adult life from 1207 to 1273. Scholars can therefore explore the sexual conventions of Rumi's day by first looking back to the deep cultural roots of the Greeks.

Many scholars believe that, in the Greek Empire, passive and active sexual roles were of primary importance when discussing sexual acts. The penetrated, or the passive partner, was deemed feminine, regardless of the sex of the person.[26] On the other hand, the penetrator played the active role and was the considered masculine.[27]

In her article arguing for the inclusion of art depicting homosexual sex, Whitney Davis writes about vase painting in the Greek Empire. She writes that many "Greek painted vases depict scenes of homosocial relationships and homosexual courtship or sexual activity and were actually made as love gifts to be passed between men."[28] She notes that an older Athenian male courted a young, passive boy and that this system was continuous, meaning the older man was once a young boy, himself, being courted. Davis writes that young Athenian men advance in this system by first taking on the "passive homosexual role, which was not supposed to provide bodily pleasure but was an accepted ritual of apprenticeship in wisdom."[29] K. J. Dover, a scholar at the forefront of the discussion on Greek homosexual behavior, writes that the "younger partner is said to 'grant favors' or 'render services'."[30] They then become the "man's adult, active homosexual role" where he reaps the benefit of his "full status as a man of affairs, of real economic, political, and sexual power."[31]

Dover also writes of the political ramifications of male-male sexual activity. If an Athenian man accepted money in exchange for sexual favors, he was stripped of his voting rights. Dover writes that "to play the role of a prostitute was, as it were, to remove oneself from the citizen-body" since most prostitutes were non-citizens or slaves.[32]

K. A. Kapparis, however, provides a contrasting voice to the scholars who have dominated the field of Greek homosexual activity. He fervently disagrees with Dover's conclusions about Greek homosexuality, stating that Dover uses insufficient evidence to draw his conclusions about Greek homosexual love.[33] He writes, "This forced interpretation of such scanty evidence is fueled by modern taboos about anal intercourse, domination, penetration and shame, which the ancient world obviously did not share."[34] He further argues that homosexual sex was not viewed as inferior to heterosexual sex; it was "simply a matter of preference."[35] This particular view of Greek homosexuality also diverges from the prevailing view of passive-active roles in sex.

Kapparis claims that the Athenian state avoided legislating the morals of its citizen-body, "so long as their actions did not interfere with important issues of public life."[36] He writes that in Athens, the (free) people may do whatever they please so long as it does not infringe upon the common good.[37]

The prevailing scholars who study Ancient Greece and Premodern Islam discuss the sexual roles each party plays, in other words, the active or passive roles. Kapparis does not agree with this widely accepted view, in part because of the lack of evidence. But El-Rouayheb offers evidence within a legal context that a man playing the passive role might have actually had a consequence within pre-modern Islam.

Homosexual relations in pre-modern Islam

In the pre-modern Islamic world, "religiously sanctioned marriage, the patriarchal household, reproductive imperatives, and women's enclosure within domestic space" functioned as the norm, according to Babayan and Afsaneh.[38] However, El-Rouayheb argues that the "heterosexual libido was blocked in [the] premodern Middle East" due to factors such as public gender segregation and arranged marriages.[39] This implies that homosexual activity not only had plenty of space to thrive, but that heterosexual relations might have been suppressed. Indeed, male-male sexual encounters were typically between an older man and a young beardless boy or between two men, one of whom is portrayed as afflicted and pathological.[40] As a result, male-male sexual relations are prevalent in Islamic literature, and homosexual activity is clearly evident by the sheer number of legal cases addressing it, but that does not imply its acceptance in society.

Sex, whether it is heterosexual or homosexual, can be viewed either as a unifying experience or as "deeply polarizing…distinguish[ing] the dominating from the dominated."[41] This aggressive view is evident early in the Ottoman Empire, where male success was intricately tied to his gender role. "Succeeding in this world was to succeed as a male, to live up to the demands of masculinity."[42] When one man comes out on top, another man loses. The winner metaphorically "screws" the loser, robbing him of his chance to succeed at being a good man, thus feminizing him.[43] While this "screwing" was not sexual in action, it contains explicit sexual undertones between men.

In the pre-modern Middle East, there was also symbolic significance tied to the act of male homosexual activity: anal intercourse. The penetrator, or the lūṭī, was the more dominant party. The term derives from the story of Lot (Arabic: *Lūt*) in the Qur'an which features sodomized boys and anally raped male trespassers.[44]

In Shari'a law, a *lūtī* is a man who commits *liwāt*, anal intercourse with another man regardless of the role he played (active or passive).[45] In the thirteenth-century epic *Sīrat Baybars*, originating in Egypt, a *lūtī* describes adult men "who make sexual advances to beardless youths."[46] According to Shi'a scholar Muhammad al-Hurr al-'Āmilī, a *lūtī* traditionally refers to a man who sodomizes boys, where sodomy refers to a "crime against nature."[47] This included anal or oral intercourse between humans or between a human and an animal.[48] The key difference between these two definitions of a *lūtī* is the age of the actors. Shari'a law describes a *lūtī* as a man engaging in intercourse with another man, while Shi'a scholar al-Hurr al-'Āmilī posits that a *lūtī* a man who has intercourse with a young boy. Both cases are represented in the literature.

While a *lūtī* was punished by the courts, a man who desired anal sex was punished socially. Those who desired penetration were called *mukhannath, ma'būn,* or *'ilq*.[49] The *ma'būn* was believed to be suffering from a disease called *ubnah*, which was a popular idea throughout the later Ottoman Empire.[50] "Treatise on the Hidden Illness," a medical journal attributed to Ar-Razi (854-925), was the first comprehensive report on *ubnah*.[51] *Ubnah* was believed to be inherited or spread through anal penetration. It was an anal itch that made you seek and desire anal intercourse.[52] The person afflicted with *ubnah* was typically effeminate with certain distinguishable characteristics, such as a "languid look, dried lips, and a large posterior."[53] These accounts describe a man who desires anal intercourse.

However, most male-male sexual activity documented in the literature did not fall within the aforementioned category. Homosexual relations in medieval Islam were almost always between a man and a young beardless boy.[54] When asked why homosexuality was forbidden, the Prophet Muhammad's son-in-law 'Ali answered that if men were permitted to sleep with beardless boys, they would not desire women and would no longer procreate.[55] The boy is referred to as *amrad* (beardless boy), *ghulām* or *sabī* (boy), *fatā, shābb,* or *hadath* (male youth).[56] Because of his lack of a beard, he was not yet culturally or socially regarded as a "man." Stature and honor was asserted by facial hair throughout history, from the Greek Empire through the Ottoman Empire, and it was deeply related to masculinity.[57] El-Rouayheb writes that male youths' visible lack of a beard was emphasized even more heavily because women normally covered their features with veils in public.[58] Gender segregation in the pre-modern period did not inhibit male-male sexual encounters the way it did with heterosexual suitors. However, if the pursued boy "display[ed] too much enthusiasm for his role as a coveted object," it was at the peril of his own reputation.[59]

According to Bruce W. Dunne, "lawful sexual intercourse" in Islam exists only between a woman and a man, but one can infer from the remaining literature and Islamic holy texts that homosexual activity occurred throughout the pre-modern Islamic world.[60] For the woman, lawful sex means sex with "her husband only, for the man [it is] with his wives and slave girls."[61] Dunne also notes the condemnation of sodomy in the Qur'an and hadith, implying that male-male sexual intercourse happened at the time in which both of these religious works were composed, estimated to be in the seventh-century CE.

Texts
Sexual imagery in Rumi's writings
Rumi's primary life works are *Dīwān Shamsi Tabrīzī* and *Mathnawī*.[62] It is important to note that Shams is not directly mentioned in every story or stanza of these works, but all of Rumi's poetry is addressed to his spiritual guide. This is an extraordinary testament to his teacher, as the *Dīwān Shamsi Tabrīzī*, also referred to simply as *Dīwān*, itself contains more than 40,000 verses, which is well beyond the scope to include within this article.

Rumi has therefore written thousands of verses, some about sex between men and women and some about sexual encounters between two men. Scholars in the field of mysticism studies have amply addressed the sexual nature of Rumi's poetry. Mahdi Tourage specifically finds that "crude imagery and tales must be considered as indispensable to the mystical significance of the *Mathnawī*."[63] This crude imagery includes sexual interactions with both married and unmarried women and even between humans and animals. One such case is the story of the slave girl and the donkey in *Mathnawī*. One translation of the story begins as follows:

> There was a maidservant
>
> who had cleverly trained a donkey
>
> to perform the services of a man.[64]

The maidservant trained the donkey to have sexual intercourse with her. In order to avoid injury, she created a protective device from a gourd to cover the donkey's penis. The mistress saw the maidservant and the donkey together, and she wanted to experience that pleasure for herself. She sent the maidservant away and attempted to have sex with the donkey, ultimately resulting in her bloody death.

> The maidservant returns and says, "Yes, you saw
>
> my pleasure, but you didn't see the gourd
>
> that put a limit on it. You opened
>
> your shop before a Master
>
> taught you the craft.[65]

Rumi teaches his reader the importance of balance and knowledge. He warns against indulging oneself in absolute pleasure without first seeking knowledge. Had the mistress known about the gourd, sexual intercourse with the donkey would not have resulted in her death. However, she simply saw the act taking place and made her own assessment of the situation without first asking for the maidservant's guidance. She prioritized pleasure over knowledge, and the result was fatal. Although the story is vulgar, it contains a lesson and a deep meaning. Rumi's poetry often takes this style.

Academics have also directly addressed the homoerotic themes in Rumi's poetry. El-Rouayheb writes of Rumi's personal relationships with his mother-in-law and her family, which were so tumultuous that they lead to his divorce from his wife. At the end of his work *Dīwān Shamsi-Tabrīzī*, Rumi writes that he is going to avoid women altogether once his marriage ends and pursue beardless men, according to El-Rouayheb.[66]

Rumi also writes about a sexual encounter between a man and young boy in his work *Mathnawī*.

> The man said: Don't be afraid, my beautiful boy!
>
> If you want, you can be also on the top!
>
> If you are afraid of me, you should know that I am a
>
> *mokhannas* [a passive homosexual],
>
> So sit on me and ride me as if I was a camel![67]

This passage highlights the crude nature of Rumi's poetry. While readers today cannot extrapolate biographical information from such a vague excerpt, and therefore cannot know who Rumi was referring to in this passage, we are able to infer that he was writing about a man and a young boy. Many scholars would deem the older man more masculine since he was typically the penetrator and the dominant party. However, Rumi writes that this man is willing to concede his masculinity by letting the boy, considered by many to be effeminate until showing a beard, "ride [him] as if [he were] a camel."[68] This excerpt shows that active/passive sexual roles perhaps were not as defined as some scholars may have believed. This poem implies that there is more fluidity in the roles one party performs, and it may change per act or per partner. For example, Rumi writes that the man said the boy may "also be on top."[69] This can be read as the man telling the boy that he is comfortable being penetrated by him instead of what might have been typical during male-male sex; it could also mean that the man consents to both penetrating the boy and being penetrated by the boy; in other words, both parties will perform both roles during the encounter.

Rumi writes much of his poetry in ghazal verse. A *ghazal* is a form of Arabic love-themed poetry that is often sung.[70] Many verses of this nature are written to unidentified persons. Rumi writes in ghazal to both men and women in an "unseemly and indecorous" nature.[71] One example is when Rumi responds to those who made fun of him for being effeminate:

> May God punish everyone who says that I am effeminate
>
> By my sleeping with his mother for one night- not for three.
>
> If he were to see--watched man!--how her field is ploughed.
>
> While she blazed and panted at the heat of my glans.
>
> He would know whether it was a man or a woman who covered her.[72]

Here, Rumi writes in the first-person narrative. While we cannot know if he was actually referring to himself when writing this passage, Rumi does convey a certain appetite for revenge when a man, "I" in the passage, is referred to as "effeminate" in this selection.[73] It is also noteworthy that the means of revenge is of the sexual nature, as opposed to violence, for example. Rumi could have threatened to harm anyone who called him, the "I' in the passage, feminine; instead, he chose to assert his masculinity by threatening to have sex with their mother(s).

This poem lends credence to El-Rouayheb's view of pre-modern Islam where masculinity was connected to success through gender roles. The man Rumi writes about seeks to disprove his femininity by demonstrating his masculinity. He does so by threatening to dominate people's mothers and therefore succeed at what is expected of him as a man.

Rumi again writes of sexual activity, but this encounter is with a boy:

> Many a boy, whose face did not disgrace him...
>
> ...Sometimes I make him kneel down, Sometimes I lay him on his front
>
> Sometimes I lay him on his back
>
> Both curing him of his illness and wounding him.
>
> With a full glans that pierces him like a weapon.[74]

Rumi is again using the first-person narrative in this excerpt when writing about sexual intercourse with a young boy. The illness Rumi might have been alluding to is *ubnah*, which was discussed previously.[75] If Rumi was in fact referring to *ubnah*, then the implication, at least within the context of pre-modern Middle East, is that the boy actively desired anal penetration. From the context, one might infer that the man from who's perspective Rumi is writing was the active, insertive, dominant party and the boy was the passive, vulnerable party. Further, the reader can infer that the narrator, "I" in the passage, did not pay the boy for sex because the boy actively desired it. In this case, the sexual encounter is more closely related to *ma'būn* as opposed to *lūtī*.

Rumi writes explicitly of sexual encounters both between men and women and between men and boys. The encounters he describes are crude in nature, but often contain a lesson, such as the poem about the donkey. Rumi's poetry about Shams-Tabrizi, on the other hand, is much more longing and loving. Shams is the physical embodiment of God on earth for Rumi since Shams is his spiritual master. Rumi's poetry reflects his desire and longing for God, which manifests as his adoration for his master.

Rumi's Love Poetry to His Master

It is well established that Rumi wrote sexual poetry about men and women alike. But Rumi's poetry to Shams is much different from any sexual writings previously discussed; the love Rumi had for his master transcends any sexual relationship, and it is evident in Rumi's writings.

In one of the verses Rumi speaks of Shams, he writes of him lovingly:

> You are the bait and the trap/ You are the path and the map/ While in search I remain
>
> You are poison and the sweet/ You are defeated and defeat/ Sword in hand I remain
>
> You are the wood and the saw/ You are cooked, and are raw/ While in a pot I remain
>
> You are sunshine and the fog/ You are water and the jug/ While thirsty I remain
>
> Sweet fragrance of Shams is/ The joy and pride of Tabriz/ Perfume trader I remain."[76]

Rumi again writes of the necessity of seeking knowledge, as he did with the story of the slave girl and the donkey.[77] The *tariqa* Rumi followed was led by Shams, his spiritual guide. Rumi remained eager to learn until *fana* was achieved. The first line of the above stanza is "I need a lover and a friend/All friendships you transcend."[78] As Rumi's master and personification of God, Shams-Tabrizi transcended friendship and became much closer with Rumi as Rumi followed the *tariqa*. Shams-Tabrizi encompasses all aspects of Rumi's life, from sunshine to fog to poison to sweetness. All the while, Rumi remains in search for the answers that only Shams is able to provide him, ultimately providing him with the tools necessary to achieve *fana*. Rumi is vulnerable in his relationship with Shams because only Shams can fill the void missing in Rumi's life and answer his many questions.

Rumi again writes of Shams in the *Dīwān*, this time speaking of his physical appearance:

> This hidden face, gorgeous lashes
>
> The arched brow, eye that flashes
>
> The moving brow and talking eye I know not, I know not
>
> Powerful arm, the nimble bow,
>
> Put in flight temporal arrow

> Bow and arrow and arm and time I know not, I know not
>
> Shams-e Tabrizi, to you I'm brought
>
> With your hardness I am distraught
>
> That shining gem, this hard rock, I know not, I know not.[79]

The line "I know not" repeated might indicate the apophatic knowledge that Rumi seeks to gain through his spiritual master. Rumi recognizes his own ignorance and inability to achieve *fana* without the help of Shams, which is why he emphasizes the pursuit of knowledge in a great deal of his poetry.

In this passage, Rumi writes of Shams' physical appearance, mentioning his lashes and arms. It is possible that, at this point, Rumi had already achieved *fana*; but because of mystical experience's ineffable quality, he was unable to describe the experience itself. Instead, he describes his spiritual master who taught him the *tariqa* and represents everything he has come to understand about Sufism and the divine.

After an unknown yet uninterrupted period of time spent alone with Rumi, Shams-Tabrizi vanished. As previously stated, no one can be sure exactly what came of Shams-Tabrizi after he left Rumi, whether he was murdered or if he simply left Konia.[80] Regardless of Shams-Tabrizi's fate, he was gone from Rumi's life forever. Rumi wrote poetry of his absence, longing for his spiritual master:

> Thy face is spring like, thy fire sorrows fight
>
> How long burn in this solstice of separation, candle-like?
>
> From the memory of thy light, every night flames take flight
>
> If only my heart fire would burn, my soul desire candle-like.
>
> How long burn thyself Shams-e Tabrizi, thy love beaming bright
>
> We know of nothing other than burning up, candle-like.[81]

In this stanza, Rumi aches for Shams' return, unknowing if he will ever come back to Konia. He begins by again admiring Shams' appearance, noting that it is "spring like," and wonders how long the two will be apart.[82] He writes of Shams' positive qualities, noting that he is a "fire" that fights away sorrow and describes him as a "light" and "candle-like."[83] Rumi writes, "How long burn in this solstice of separation."[84] It is possible that Shams left Rumi because he knew Rumi needed to continue to follow the path on his own, unhindered by a master.

Rumi could have written this passage about Shams' absence. Rumi could also have a deeper aching and longing for God. Shams embodied God for Rumi, and one day Rumi woke up and Shams was gone. Rumi was left to attempt to achieve *fana* all on his own. This passage could be interpreted as Rumi expressing his adoration and yearning for God through Shams-Tabrizi. Rumi never learned what came of Shams, so he might have spent his entire life aching from this separation.

Conclusion

Rumi is one of the most well-recognized mystics in Islam, as his poetry has gained renown across the globe. His spiritual master Shams-Tabrizi has less name recognition, though he was extremely important to Rumi's development as a prominent Sufi poet.

This article has examined the social roles of ancient Greece and premodern Islam that provide cultural contexts for Rumi's poetry. Most scholars in the field write that active and passive sexual roles were tied to masculinity and femininity, respectively, and that whomever was penetrated was deemed feminine and whomever was penetrating was deemed masculine, regardless of sex. Davis and Dover write that male-male sex was cyclical and transactional in ancient Greece,[85] and they describe a normalized culture of older men providing insight and wisdom to young boys in exchange for sex. Kapparis rejects this view as well as the larger view of active/passive roles, and writes that the ancient Greeks did not have much regard for who slept with whom, so long as they performed their duties to uphold the common good.[86]

This article then discussed male-male sex in pre-modern Islam and the potential consequences that followed. A man having sex with men or boys, depending on the legal system, is a called a *lūtī* and is punished by the courts. A *ma'būn* was punished socially, as he was a man who actively desired anal sex and was believed to be afflicted with a disease called *ubnah*.[87] Rumi even alludes to *ubnah* in one of his poems about a man and a boy, where the man is "curing him [the boy] of his illness" with anal penetration.[88]

The manner in which Rumi writes his sexual poetry, regardless of the parties involved, is typically crude, vulgar, and extremely detailed. Rumi also wrote countless passages about his master Shams, his embodiment of the divine. While this homoerotic poetry contained some mention of Shams' physical appearance, it did not compare to the vulgarity of the sexual poetry Rumi wrote about other individuals. The poetry written to Shams was homoerotic love poetry about a disciple eager to learn from his master and seek answers about the *tariqa*. As Shams was the means by which Rumi was able to achieve union with God, the two men became very close. But Rumi's love poetry was not only directed toward Shams, it was also for a genderless God. Shams was somewhat of a representative of the Divine as he was a spiritual master in Sufism. Rumi might not have been able to describe Allah, but he was able to admire Shams' face, brows, arms, and overall appearance. Provided the long-standing Greek conventions of male-male sexual relations in medieval Turkey, Rumi's most prevalent sexual theme is homoerotic, directed at his older, wise teacher, Shams-Tabrizi.

Notes

1. DeSouza, Wendy Noel, *Scholarly Mysticism and the Mystical Scholars: European and Iranian Intellectuals at the Dawn of Modern Sexuality and Gender* (Los Angeles: University of California, 2010).
2. Losensky, Paul, 2009, "Poetics and Eros in Early Modern Persia: The Lovers' Confection and The Glorious Epistle by Muhtasham Kāshānī." *Iranian Studies* pp. 745-764.
3. El-Zein, Amira, Spiritual Consumption in the United States: The Rumi Phenomenon (Routledge, 2000), p. 71.
4. Underhill, Evelyn, *Mysticism: A Study in the Nature and Development of Man's Spiritual Consciousness* (London: Methuen & Co., 1912), p. 138.
5. El-Zein. "Spiritual Consumption in the United States...," 71.
6. Ibid.
7. Ibid.; Rumi is not the only one to have adopted the name of his country as his own. Shams-Tabrizi appears to have done the same. Shams is from Tabriz, one of the largest cities in Iran.
8. Lewis, Franklin D., *Rumi: Past and Present, East and West: the Life, Teaching and Poetry of Jalâl Al-Din Rumi* (Oxford: Oneworld, 2003), p. 272.
9. Ibid, 273.
10. Ibid.
11. Ibid.
12. Lewis. *Rumi: Past and Present, East and West...*, 274; El-Zein. "Spiritual Consumption in the United States...," 71.
13. Lewis. *Rumi: Past and Present, East and West...*, 274.
14. Katz, Steven, *Understanding Mysticism: Mysticism and Philosophical Analysis* (Oxford University Press, 1978), p. 44.
15. Ibid.
16. Underhill. *Mysticism: A Study in the Nature...*,138.

17. Tabrīzī, Shams-i, *Me & Rumi: The Autobiography of Shams-i Tabrizi* (Independent Publishing Group, 2004), p. 185.
18. Ibid, 186.
19. Ibid, 212.
20. El-Zein. "Spiritual Consumption in the United States....," 71.
21. Shiva, Shahram. 2018. *Rumi's Untold Story: From 30-Year Research.* Rumi Network.
22. Ibid.
23. Karras, Ruth Mazo, 2000, "Active/Passive, Acts/Passions: Greek and Roman Sexualities," *The American Historical Review* (Oxford University Press), p. 1251.
24. Ibid, 1252.
25. Patrikarakos, David, 2015, *POLITICO.* April 22. https://www.politico.eu/article/the-greeks-are-not-western/. accessed on April 2019.
26. Karras. "Active/Passive, Acts/Passions...," 1255, 1256.
27. Ibid.
28. Davis, Whitney, 1992, "Founding the Closet: Sexuality and the Creation of Art History." *Art Documentation: Journal of the Art Libraries Society of North America*: 171.
29. Ibid.
30. Dover, K. J., 1973, "CLASSICAL GREEK ATTITUDES TO SEXUAL BEHAVIOR." *Arethusa*: 67.
31. Davis. "FOUNDING THE CLOSET...," 171.
32. Dover. "CLASSICAL GREEK ATTITUDES...," 68.
33. Kapparis, Konstantinos, *Prostitution in the Ancient Greek World* (de Gruyter, 2017), p. 198.
34. Ibid.
35. Ibid, 199.
36. Ibid, 193.
37. Ibid, 204.
38. Najmabadi, Kathryn, Afsaneh Babayan, *Islamicate Sexualities: Translations across Temporal Geographies of Desire* (Harvard University Center for Middle Eastern Studies, 2008), p. 23.
39. El-Rouayheb, Khaled, *Before Homosexuality in the Arab-Islamic World, 1500-1800* (University of Chicago Press, 2009), p. 30.
40. Ibid, 19, 20.
41. Ibid, 15.
42. Ibid, 25.
43. Ibid, 26.
44. El-Rouayheb. *Before Homosexuality...*, 17.
45. Ibid, 16.
46. Ibid.
47. Ibid, 17.
48. n.d. *The Free Dictionary.* https://legal-dictionary.thefreedictionary.com/sodomy. accessed on March 2018.
49. El-Rouayheb. *Before Homosexuality...*, 16.
50. Ibid.
51. Dunne, Bruce W., 1990, "Homosexuality in the Middle East: An Agenda for Historical Research." *Arab Studies Quarterly*, pp. 58.
52. El-Rouayheb. *Before Homosexuality...*, 19, 20.

53. Ibid, 20.
54. Ibid, 26.
55. Ibid, 16.
56. Ibid.
57. Ibid, 26, 27.
58. Ibid, 27.
59. Ibid.
60. Dunne. "Homosexuality in the Middle East…," 64.
61. Ibid.
62. El-Zein. "Spiritual Consumption in the United States…," 71.
63. Tourage, Mahdi, *Rūmī and the Hermeneutics of Eroticism* (Leiden: BRILL, 2007), pp. 28.
64. sumnun. n.d. *alpha naseeb*. http://www.naseeb.com/journals/very-interesting-rumi-poem-x-rated-7756. accessed on April 2018.
65. Ibid.
66. El-Rouayheb. *Before Homosexuality…*, 29.
67. O'Connell, Barry, 2015, *Young boys as Sexual Objects in Persian Art*. January 29. http://islamic-art-jboc.blogspot.com/2015/01/young-boys-as-sexual-objects-in-persian.html. accessed on April 2018.
68. Ibid.
69. Ibid.
70. 2014. *Ghazal: Poetic Form* . February 20. https://poets.org/text/ghazal-poetic-form. accessed on March 2018.
71. El-Huni, Ali A., *The poetry of Ibn al-Rùmī* (University of Glasgow, 1996), p. 302.
72. Ibid, 39.
73. Ibid.
74. Ibid, 45.
75. See page 5.
76. Shahriari, Shahriar, *Divan-e Shams & Translations from Divan-e Shams,* 1998. Vancouver, July 20.
77. See Page 6.
78. Shahriari. *Divan-e Shams & Translations…*
79. Ibid.
80. Shiva. *Rumi's Untold Story…*
81. Shahriari. *Divan-e Shams & Translations…*
82. Ibid.
83. Ibid.
84. Ibid.
85. Davis. "FOUNDING THE CLOSET…," 171; Dover. "CLASSICAL GREEK ATTITUDES…," 67.
86. Kapparis. *Prostitution in the Ancient Greek World*, 204.
87. El-Rouayheb. *Before Homosexuality…*, 16.
88. El-Huni. *The poetry of Ibn al-Rùmī*, 41; See page 7.

Works Cited

Davis, Whitney, 1992, "Founding the Closet: Sexuality and the Creation of Art History," Art Documentation: Journal of the Art Libraries Society of North America **11**(4), pp. 171–75.

DeSouza, Wendy Noel, 2010, Scholarly Mysticism and the Mystical Scholars: European and Iranian Intellectuals at the Dawn of Modern Sexuality and Gender. Los Angeles: University of California.

Dover, KJ., 1973, "Classical Greek attitudes to sexual behavior," Arethusa **6**, pp. 59–73.

Dunne, Bruce W., 1990, "Homosexuality in the Middle East: An Agenda for Historical Research," Arab Studies Quarterly **12**, pp. 55–83.

El-Huni, Ali A., 1996, The Poetry of Ibn al-Rùmi. Glasgow: University of Glasgow.

El-Rouayheb, Khaled, 2009, Before Homosexuality in the Arab-Islamic World, 1500–1800. Chicago: University of Chicago Press.

El-Zein, Amira, 2000, "Spiritual Consumption in the United States: The Rumi phenomenon," Islam and Christian–Muslim Relations **11** (1), pp. 71–85.

Ghazal: Poetic Form, 2014, February 20. https://poets.org/text/ghazal-poetic-form. accessed on March 2018.

Kapparis, Konstantinos, 2017, Prostitution in the Ancient Greek World. Berlin, Germany: de Gruyter.

Karras, Ruth Mazo, 2000, "Active/Passive, Acts/Passions: Greek and Roman Sexualities," The American Historical Review (Oxford University Press) **105**, 1250–1265.

Katz, Steven, 1978, Understanding Mysticism: Mysticism and Philosophical Analysis. Oxford: Oxford University Press.

Lewis, Franklin D., 2003, Rumi: Past and Present, East and West: the Life, Teaching and Poetry of Jalâl Al-Din Rumi, Oxford: Oneworld.

Losensky, Paul, 2009, "Poetics and Eros in Early Modern Persia: The Lovers' Confection and The Glorious Epistle by Muhtasham Kāshānī," Iranian Studies **42**, pp. 745–764.

Najmabadi, Kathryn, Afsaneh Najmabadi, 2008, Islamicate Sexualities: Translations across Temporal Geographies of Desire. Cambridge: Harvard University Center for Middle Eastern Studies.

O'Connell, Barry, 2015, Young boys as Sexual Objects in Persian Art. January 29. http://islamic-art-jboc.blogspot.com/2015/01/young-boys-as-sexual-objects-in-persian.html. Accessed on April 2018.

Patrikarakos, David, 2015, POLITICO. April 22. https://www.politico.eu/article/the-greeks-are-not-western/. Accessed on April 2019.

Shahriari, Shahriar, 1998, Divan-e Shams & Translations from Divan-e Shams. Vancouver, July 20.

Shiva, Shahram, 2018, Rumi's Untold Story: From 30-Year Research. Rumi Network.

sumnun, n.d. alpha naseeb. http://www.naseeb.com/journals/very-interesting-rumi-poem-x-rated-7756. accessed on April 2018.

Tabrīzī, Shams-i, 2004, Me & Rumi: The Autobiography of Shams-i Tabrizi. Chicago, IL: Independent Publishing Group.

n.d. The Free Dictionary, 2018, https://legal-dictionary.thefreedictionary.com/sodomy. accessed on March 2018.

Tourage, Mahdi, 2007, Rūmī and the Hermeneutics of Eroticism, Leiden: BRILL.

Underhill, Evelyn, 1912, Mysticism: A Study in the Nature and Development of Man's Spiritual Consciousness, London: Methuen & Co.

CROSSCURRENTS

LEAH AND HAGAR
An Intergenerational Conversation of Belonging

Ashley Starr-Morris

Introduction

The God of Abraham, Isaac, and Jacob. This is the patriarchal recitation and reminder of the biblical covenant with the Deity. But what about the God of Sarah, Rebekah, and Rachel? These matriarchs are too often neglected in not only the stories of the Torah, but in theology, historical analysis, academic work, and exegetical commentary. They have a less significant role, with no place of their own in the androcentric confines of the Abrahamic religions. So then, if these matriarchs are dominated by the reigning men of the Hebrew Bible, where do other women fit into the story? What about the God of Hagar, Leah, Bilhah, and Zilpah? What of these "less significant" women—the women who are hated, mistreated, and abandoned in the biblical text?

In recent feminist scholarship, there has been a concerted effort to bring more attention to these women and create a space where their roles, lives, dreams, heartaches, and deaths are explored by scholars.[1] Alice Bach, Tikva Frymer-Kensky, and Phyllis Trible lift up numerous women of the Bible to intentionally remember and revitalize their oft overlooked contributions and negotiate feminist ways of approaching ancient texts. In her newest work, Nyasha Junior offers a reception history of Hagar as a Black woman, examining the influence of cultural-historical interpretation of Hagar in Black communities. Tammi J. Schneider finds that a closer reading of the text challenges hegemonic readings and interpretations of women; revealing Hagar, for example, to be embodied by opposites—slave and free, oppressed and favored by the Deity—making her a highly complex figure that is emblematic of the human condition.[2] Jerry Rabow weaves together interpretations of Leah found in the biblical text and midrash to expose a much fuller and more heroic picture of the commonly forgotten matriarch.

This article seeks to contribute to this same scholarship of recognition by focusing on two seemingly unrelated women: Leah, the "unloved" (Gen. 29:31) wife of Jacob, and Hagar, Sarah's slave[3] and mother to Abraham's firstborn son. In Genesis 29-31, Leah is the woman that Jacob, son of Isaac, is deceived into marrying after serving seven years for marriage to Leah's younger sister, Rachel. After Jacob marries Rachel as well, Rachel grapples with infertility for many years while Leah is able to have many children. Both Leah and Rachel also have children through their maids, Zilpah and Bilhah respectively. Hagar's story is found in Genesis 16-18 and 21, where she is given to Abraham by Sarai, her sterile owner, to provide a son in fulfillment of the covenant established with the Deity in Genesis 15. Upon conceiving, Hagar is mistreated by Sarai and flees, until the Deity instructs her to return to Sarai. Ultimately, Sarah births Isaac, completing the covenant, and Hagar and Ishmael are banished from Abraham's house permanently.[4]

The striking resemblances between their stories throw into sharp relief the connection between the two women and force a reconsideration of how these stories have historically been read. In reading these epics together, light shines on the other and an intergenerational conversation forms between two unwanted women. Bernadette Brooten enjoins scholars researching women to "place women at the center of the frame" and that by doing so "a different constellation of...cultural milieu and social world will emerge."[5] Traditional scholarship that even mentions Leah and Hagar understands them adjacent almost exclusively to Jacob and Abraham. This article seeks to intentionally put Leah and Hagar at the "center of the frame."

Three distinct categories serve as a useful structure with which to explore the two matriarchs: their relationships with the other wives; their relationships with their husbands, the patriarchs; and lastly, their relationships with the Deity. The first category will explore interrelated themes with the other wives, such as fertility and sterility; jealousy and perceptions of threat; and an ensuing competition for children. The second category will address Leah and Hagar's relationship to their husbands, evaluating areas such as the women's (un)desirability in the eyes of their husbands; issues around firstborn sons; and chosenness, sex relations, and feminine agency. The last category of analysis will examine the matriarchs' relationship to the Deity in the ways the Deity interacts with them and, at times, the ambivalent nature of the Deity's care for Leah and Hagar.

Relationship to the co-wife
Leah and Hagar are characters that stand in relation to others, rarely standing independently as their own person. Even as Leah is first introduced as a character in Genesis 29:16, she is described as the elder daughter of Laban and older sister to Rachel.[6] In Genesis 16:1, the same pattern emerges as Hagar is introduced to the reader through her position and her functionality: "Now Sarai, Abram's wife, bore him no children. She had an Egyptian slave-girl whose name was Hagar." Since Leah and Hagar's relationship with the other wife is so prominent, this is the first relationship to be considered.

Fertility and sterility are main themes that circulate Leah and Hagar's connection to their co-wives. Genesis 29:31 states, "When the Lord saw that Leah was unloved, he opened her womb." Leah's womb is opened by the Deity due precisely to her subordinate, even hated, status in the polygamous marriage between Leah, Rachel, and Jacob, while Rachel continues to struggle with sterility (29:31). Rachel appeals angrily to Jacob for not providing her with children and he rebukes her asking, "Am I in the place of God, who has withheld from you the fruit of the womb?" (30:2). It is clear in these passages that the Deity alone is the arbiter of fertility and barrenness.

Nyasha Junior shares that Hagar's narrative includes "tension between multiple characters, and highlights questions of ethnicity, age, fertility, inheritance, [and] obedience," making an excellent model for "concerns regarding inclusion and exclusion."[7] This unique situatedness is exemplified from the beginning of Hagar's polycoity[8] relationship, as her only pathway to becoming Abram's wife is strictly through her owner's sterility (16:1). Hagar is more an instrument than a person; her sole role is to build up her mistress through her supposed fecundity.[9] Genesis 16:2 reveals Sarai's intention behind providing Abram with her slave, not to procure him a son or even to fulfill the covenant, but to provide herself with children. Sarai is her own concern as it pertains to bearing a future generation, yet again instrumentalizing Hagar's body. The reader also never sees Sarai speak directly to Hagar nor even refer to her by name, perpetuating the intentional distancing between the two wives first created by the utilization of Hagar's reproductive system.

Both of these women are defined by their ability to bear children to the patriarch, and defined over and against the other wife's inability to do so. In that sense, the Deity, "ensures the fertility of the unloved while restricting it for the loved so that no woman has the full gamut of joy and fortune."[10] This is their explicit role to fulfill in the polygamous marriages, but it does not necessarily follow that their lives are elevated by fulfilling this role.

In a reversal of traditional sensibilities, the value and honor that would normally be bestowed upon a wife who bears sons instead harnesses contempt on Leah and Hagar, increasing their burdens. Rachel's jealousy of Leah increases with every child Leah brings forth, and functions as the motivation for Rachel giving her slave, Bilhah, to Jacob in order to create a lineage for herself (Gen. 30:1, 8). The text mentions twice that Leah is hated, but it is unclear as to who is doing the hating—Rachel or Jacob or both. The text is clear, however, that Leah has earned Rachel's envy and that Rachel intends to best her sister however she can.

The discord in relationships continues with Hagar's affliction at the hands of Sarai. Cuneiform texts of the second and first millennia B.C.E. attest to the custom of using a female slave to bear children for a sterile wife. A marriage contract from Anatolia dating to around 1900 B.C.E. stipulates that the wife will buy a slave woman for the husband if the wife does not provide a child within two years.[11] Although Hagar is essentially a "womb-with-legs"[12] she does not reflexively see herself in that reductionist light, as evidenced by the way she "looked with contempt on her mistress" upon conceiving (16:4). Sarai views Hagar's attitude toward her as threatening, especially considering her place in the family as the barren wife. Hagar is the object of Sarai's wrath—voracious enough that Hagar's preferred option is to flee the household in the middle of her pregnancy (16:6).[13] Leah and Hagar incur the acrimony of the other wife in the process of fulfilling their larger roles as son-bearing-wives, caught at the nexus of a veritable quagmire.

Lastly, there exists a competition around babies that neither Leah nor Hagar seem particularly interested in, but one with which the co-wives are quite preoccupied. The text never shows Leah obsessing over having the first son before Rachel, or even more children than Rachel.[14] In fact, according to midrash about Leah's last birth, a daughter named Dinah, Leah specifically prays that the baby is a girl so that Rachel may conceive and bear a son.[15] In Genesis 30:18, Leah's motivation for giving her slave, Zilpah, to Jacob is in hopes of having more children, not to participate in the race for children but to win the heart of Jacob. In contrast, Rachel equates having no children to death, and Leah is clearly the nucleus around which Rachel's longing for children oscillates (30:1). Rachel chooses to rectify her situation by providing her slave, Bilhah, to Jacob so that Rachel may "have children through her" (30:3-4). Since Jacob already has children *vis-à-vis* Leah, Rachel is not obligated to do this.[16] This supports the argument that Rachel's desire to have children is more personally motivated; centered more firmly on the fertility competition with her sister than on securing a lineage for Jacob. Again, this impetus is repeated when Rachel quickly declares victory over Leah upon the birth of Bilhah's second son, naming him Naphtali, or "I have prevailed." Rachel affirms, "With mighty wrestlings I have wrestled with my sister, and have prevailed" (Gen. 30:8), despite Leah having four children, and four sons at that.

Likewise, Hagar is caught up in a race to provide Abram with children not only for progeny's sake but, more importantly, to fulfill the Deity's covenant with Abram; for until chapter 17, the Deity is not clear that the covenant will be established with the child born of Sarah. From that revelation forward, the conflict shifts from bearing children to Sarah securing Isaac's place as covenant-fulfiller and inheritance-receiver over Hagar's child, Ishmael. As is the case with Leah, the text never reveals any competitive spirit on the part of Hagar, but the text does illuminate Sarah's triumphant move as she demands Abraham to "cast out this slave woman with her son; for the son of this slave woman shall not inherit along with my son Isaac" (21:10). Leah and Hagar possess little agency with whom they have children, both in the biological sense (Jacob and Abraham) and in the household sense (Rachel and Sarah). To be the fertile wife in both of the triangles immediately sets up a dichotomy against the backdrop of the sterile primary wife, which culminates in an unwanted (on the part of Leah and Hagar) fertility contest.

Leah and Hagar's relationships with their co-wives are fraught with difficulties and complications, with "each [having] the outside perspective to the other's experience."[17] The women's lack of agency in their own lives is exhibited through the absence of choice regarding whom they marry—husband and co-wife alike. Even in their own story they are not understood as main characters with defining attributes and contributions, outside of what they can offer that the primary wife cannot. These two women successfully fulfill the expectations placed upon them by providing firstborn sons to their husbands. This would traditionally elevate their status and establish social capital, but instead, it brings them misfortune, particularly around their relationship to the other wife. Lastly, almost as a result of fulfilling their roles well, Leah and Hagar are thrust into a competition for children with the co-wife that the text does not indicate they want nor consciously participate in, but nonetheless one that contributes to their precarious situations.

Relationship to the husband

Leah and Hagar's relationship to their husbands, Jacob and Abraham, is a complicated one at best. The relationships are characterized by abandonment, issues of progeny, and a clear lack of being chosen. The husbands' treatment of Leah and Hagar demonstrates that they are not the primary wife, and their value is such that they are easily discarded—Leah emotionally and Hagar physically. Although both the women give birth to the first son of their husband, this does not afford them the approval that is to be expected. Lastly, neither of the women are chosen by their husbands to be a wife, but are inserted into the men's lives nonetheless.

Not only are Leah and Hagar not regarded favorably by their co-wives, they are also discarded by their respective husbands. Leah is abandoned in an emotional sense, as she is not loved by Jacob. This is clearly exhibited in Genesis 29:31-34, as the naming speeches of Leah's first three sons consistently revolve around the fact that she is not loved by her husband: Reuben or "See, a son," Simeon or "Because the Lord has heard that I am hated, he has given this son also", and Levi or "Now this time my husband will be joined to me, because I have borne him three sons."[18]

It is also evident that Leah is not Jacob's preferred sexual partner, since Leah has to purchase a night with Jacob from Rachel with Reuben's mandrakes (30:15). Leah turns the loss of sexual agency into its very reclamation when she uses the advantage the mandrakes provide to gain control; Leah once again reverses the traditional sexual prowess in her relationship with Jacob. In their first sexual encounter, Leah is the "knower" and not the typical "known", and Jacob is the "known" rather than the typical "knower." Here, the sexual encounter is purchased by a woman (instead of a man) and the man (not a woman) is the commodity acquired. In this instance, the woman is also the one initiating the sexual encounter (instead of a man) and the man acquiesces to what is requested of him (instead of a woman). Leah adroitly pursues a remedy for her emotional abandonment through whatever recourse is available to her, namely through the successful provision of sons and through manufacturing sexual access to Jacob.

Relatedly, Hagar is not only cast aside, she is cast *out*—twice. Sarai's mistreatment leads Hagar to flee to the wilderness of Shur the first time (Gen. 16:7-8), and the second time, she is cast out at the behest of Sarah who does not want Ishmael to inherit in the same way as her son Isaac (21:15). Hers is a very literal abandonment by the patriarch. Interestingly, Hagar's name is also never used by Abram either, representing an abandonment of her personhood by the very people who own her personhood.

While Leah longs to be accepted by her husband, this sentiment is not observed with Hagar, who reciprocally rejects her rejecter. This difference in approach may be attributed to their differing statuses in the relationship: Leah as true (yet secondary) wife, and Hagar as slave childbearer. Leah has a clearer—although still murky—relationship to the patriarch, and therefore has more invested in the success of the relationship. Hagar's even murkier standing as slave/mother-of-the-firstborn-son produces less investment, allowing room for more dissention. Through this, Hagar emerges as the true counter-weight to Abraham's distinction as a character, even more so than Sarah. She is spoken to by the Deity, as is Abraham (16:11-12; 12:1-2); her son is the receiver of a divine promise, as is Abraham's (17:20; 17:19); her son is saved by the Deity's intervention, as is Abraham's (21:19-20; 22:12); she chooses a wife for her son, as does Abraham (21:21; 22:2-4);[19] and she is the ancestor of twelve nations, as is Abraham (17:20; 35:22-26). Counterintuitively, Hagar with the title "slave" can be seen as more equivalent in relation to the patriarch than Leah with the title "wife."

Metaphorically, both Leah and Hagar are abandoned in their deaths, which reveals a lack of regard toward the women. Both of their deaths are silently passed over in the text, but both Rachel and Sarah's are specifically noted (35:18; the whole of chapter 23, respectively). Neither Leah nor Hagar hold a place of prominence in the eyes of their husbands and their (un)desirability facilitates this discarding.

Not only are Leah and Hagar deserted by their husbands, they are also divested of the traditional advantages that accompany birthing sons. Issues of progeny feature prominently in both stories, as both of the matriarchs give birth to their husbands' firstborn, and firstborn sons at that (16:15; 29:31). A woman's worth in a marriage is cemented by her reproductive capabilities, not only because it increases her husband's lineage but also owing to the economic augmentation of the family's workforce.[20] In a culture where this is held in high esteem, both Leah and Hagar should be reaping the social benefits that come with the status of being the mother of the firstborn son. However, it is clear this is not the case with Leah and Hagar. Leah understandably believes that providing Jacob a son will earn her what she most desires, Jacob's love, saying, "Surely my husband will love me now" (29:32). Instead of addressing this point, the text immediately moves on to Leah's second conception (29:33). Despite Leah giving birth to Jacob's first son, Reuben, and despite the six sons she ultimately carries and births, it is never revealed that Jacob loves her in return. By the birth of her fourth son, Judah, Leah effectively abandons this linkage between sons and love from her husband, saying, "This time I will praise the Lord" (29:35). Leah's sons are born with the job of cultivating a loving relationship between their parents in the absence of one, but the text does not reveal that this is ever accomplished.

The narrative never affirms that Hagar longs for anything except to flee from Sarai's wrath (16:7-8) and for her son to live after they are cast out of Abraham's house the final time (21:15). Although Ishmael is born under the notion that he will be Sarai and Abram's son, interestingly, Genesis 16:11 shows that this son is promised to Hagar, not Abram or Sarai. From the beginning of the story to the end, Ishmael is squarely under Hagar's jurisdiction. Despite this, Abraham has a meaningful connection with the child. Abraham advocates twice for Ishmael, pleading with the Deity, "If only Ishmael might live under your blessing!" (17:18) and again in Genesis 21:11. As Abraham fights for his son with one hand, he rejects him with the other. Both Abraham and the Deity reject Ishmael as the son who fulfills the covenant (17:19), and Abraham ultimately complies when he is called upon to eject Hagar and Ishmael from his household (21:14). In fact, it appears that Ishmael, not Hagar, is the reason behind their banishment from Abraham's house (21:9-10). As it pertains to Leah and Hagar's relationship with their husbands, successfully conceiving and bearing sons worsens their predicament instead of alleviating their difficulties, inverting the traditional cultural precept.[21]

In both narratives, Jacob and Abram play an active role in choosing their primary wife, Rachel and Sarai, and do not play such a role as it pertains to Leah and Hagar. In fact, in something resembling a perverse sort of parity, neither Leah and Hagar *nor* the patriarchs choose to marry each other. There are some differences between the two epics, however, as evidenced through a subcategory of choice, namely consent.

Regarding consent, the agency seems to lie in greater part with Leah and Abram than with Hagar and Jacob. It is speculated that Leah consents to marrying Jacob by using the signs that Rachel gives her, signs originally designed to confirm Rachel's identity to Jacob in anticipation of a scheme.[22] The details of this ploy are intended to recall Jacob's own deceit in obtaining the blessing from his blind father through mimicking his older twin brother Esau, the original beneficiary. Commenting on Jacob's deceit and Leah's ruse, Jagendorf states, "The blessing itself is like the sexual gift of the passion-blinded virgin groom to his open-eyed virgin bride…Sensual knowledge has turned out to be the opposite of true knowledge."[23] In other words, just as Jacob's identity is "confirmed" to be Esau's through tactile touch, Leah is "confirmed" to be Rachel through the tactile touch of sex; in both instances, the only knower of the truth is the deceiver. Jacob is the one who lacks consent in Leah's epic, as further evidenced by his angry statement to Laban upon finding himself married to Leah instead of Rachel: "What is this you have done to me…why then have you deceived me?" (29:25). Jacob neither chooses Leah nor consents to marrying her.

Conversely, Abram consents to sleeping with Hagar at the prompting of Sarai, even though the idea nor the desire originated with Abram (16:4). In this relationship, it is apparent that the power lies with Abram and not Hagar. Although Abram consents to take Hagar as a wife, Hagar is not actively selected in the way that Abram chooses Sarai to be his wife. Additionally, Hagar's economic status as a slave-now-wife immediately places her closer to a contemporary surrogate mother than to a wife, considering that "a secondary wife is a woman without economic standing in her husband's household."[24] This standing, or lack thereof, is further fortified when Abram returns his ownership of Hagar to Sarai, telling Sarai, "Your slave girl is in your power" (16:6); again as Abram advocates only for Ishmael and not Hagar when the Deity announces the pathway of the covenant through Sarah's child (17:18); and lastly, when Sarah demands the expulsion of Hagar and Ishmael, which is "distressing to Abraham *on account of his son*" demonstrating no regard for Hagar (emphasis mine; 21:11). Not only is Hagar repeatedly not chosen by the patriarch, she is also not chosen by the Deity. In Genesis 17:19-22, the Deity is clear that the pair of covenantal promise is Sarah and Isaac, not Hagar and Ishmael.

Although the two stories in some ways are the reverse of each other, there exists a central theme of Leah and Hagar as a secondary, unchosen, and therefore unwanted, wife. Despite the fact that they are not chosen by the patriarch and largely do not have control over what happens to their own destinies, they are active agents any time an opportunity presents itself. Leah is the "knower" instead of the "known" in each significant sexual encounter with Jacob in the biblical narrative, and is not timid about manipulating a situation that is in her favor (the mandrakes) to gain access to Jacob. Likewise, Hagar emerges as Abraham's equal in many respects and is quite active within the narrative. Although Leah and Hagar's relationships to the patriarchs are characterized by abandonment, an increase in suffering due to bearing children, and trauma by repeatedly not being chosen, they express their agency in powerful ways within their marital relationships.

Relationship to the Deity

The Deity plays a vital role in both of these epics, but one that is somewhat ambivalent. The Deity neither acts totally benevolently nor totally maliciously toward Leah and Hagar. In surveying the Deity's interactions with the two women, some prevailing patterns emerge. Both of the women have encounters with the Deity; both of the women's children play special roles in the sacred lineages of their families; and then, there is the matter of divine justice—or lack thereof. What is unmistakable is that the Deity does not ignore them, starkly contrasting the way they are largely ignored by their husbands and co-wives.

Leah and Hagar each have unique encounters with the Deity. The Deity *shämas*, or hears, each of the women; Leah is heard twice (29:33, 30:17) and Hagar is heard once (16:11). However, it is also interesting to note that Ishmael's name means "God hears"[25] and that is precisely what happens in Genesis 21:17 when the Deity hears Ishmael's cries as he and Hagar are dying in the desert. Hagar is also found by the Deity (16:7), and the Deity speaks to her twice—both of the times that she is evicted from Abraham's house (16:7, 21:16). In fact, the Deity is the first entity to speak to Hagar and use her name, thereby acknowledging what Sarai and Abram cannot—her personhood.[26] Further, she is the only woman in the Hebrew Bible to name the Deity, saying, "You are El-roi [the God who sees me]...I have now seen the One who sees me" (16:13). This is extraordinary, especially considering that she is never identified as being Jewish.[27]

What is just as remarkable are the similarities in the renaming narratives between Hagar and Abraham's encounters with the Deity. The renaming narratives both involve the promise of a multitude of offspring (16:10; 17:5-6), land (Beer-lahai-roi [Well of the Living One Who Sees Me] in 16:14; Canaan in 17:8), and the naming of a forthcoming son (Ishmael in 16:11; Isaac in 17:19). Where the parallels diverge is who, exactly, leaves the encounter with the name change: Abraham's encounter results in a name change for him (Abram to Abraham), while Hagar's story sees the Deity's name changed (El-roi).

If the parallels match so directly up to that point, what is the significance behind this reversal of the renaming? Abraham's story may provide a clue. One objective of the Deity's new name for Abraham is to bind him to the covenant and serve as a reminder to Abraham to fulfill his obligation to the covenant, namely circumcision. The same can be said for the Deity's name change. It serves to bind the Deity to the promise made to Hagar regarding Ishmael in chapter 16, and serves as an injunction to remember that promise when Ishmael lays dying in the wilderness in chapter 21. It is not Hagar that needs to be reminded, but the Deity and Abraham that require the remembrance associated with the significance of a name change.

Leah, too, is heard and seen by the Deity; however, all of the interactions produce a very specific result, a child. Leah proclaims that she has received her second son, Simeon, because the Deity heard that she is hated (29:33). The second time the Deity hears Leah it is confirmed by the narrator, with the result being a fifth son, Issachar (30:17). Leah is also seen by the Deity, and this is what enables her to conceive initially (29:31). This continues a motif of seeing and eyes that is woven throughout Leah's story. Her eyes are the only feature mentioned when she is introduced in Genesis 29. As previously discussed, this idea of seeing is dripping with irony, as Jacob first deceived his father, who could not see, to obtain the blessing meant for his older twin brother, and in turn was deceived by Leah when he could not see the night of their marriage. These two secondary wives encounter the Deity in ways that the primary wives do not; this signals their value to the Deity and should reframe their significance in each narrative.

Not only is their significance revealed in their encounters with the Deity, but also with their positionality as matriarchs in consequential lineages. Leah and Hagar each contribute significantly to the unfolding of the divine lineage in the Hebrew Bible. Leah gives birth to *half* of the tribes of Israel (35:23), which increases to two-thirds if Zilpah's children are counted as Leah's (35:26). She is also the mother of Judah, who features prominently in Jewish tradition as the notable Tribe of Judah and as part of the messianic patrilineal line in Christianity.

Hagar has only one child, Ishmael, who is an influential character in his own right. He is the first son of Abraham, born to fulfill the covenantal prophecy before the Deity clarifies the matrilineal line. He is also considered the father of the Arab people according to Islamic tradition.[28] The Deity also establishes a separate promise with Ishmael in which the Deity "will surely bless him," giving him many descendants who will become "a great nation" (17:20). Schneider notes that with this promise, Hagar is elevated to the same level as all the patriarchs.[29] She is the "only woman to receive a divine promise of seed, not through a man but as her own destiny."[30] Additionally, while Ishmael does not inherit in the same way as Isaac, he still inherits, notably not through his father but through his mother.[31] Leah and Hagar are the progenitors of key figures in the Hebrew Bible, and their bodies are the arena upon which this divine drama is enacted.

In these epics, the Deity "appears to be promoting the affairs of families and nations through the happy and natural combination of male weakness and female intelligence, resourcefulness and fertility."[32] Without these women's ability to conceive, successfully birth, and then raise their sons, the epic would not continue. Their bodies creating and sustaining life is sharply juxtaposed to their co-wives enduring (but eventually overturned) sterility. The text reveals that the Deity was involved in Leah (29:31) and Hagar's conceptions (16:11) just as the Deity caused Sarah (21:1-2) and Rachel (30:22) to conceive. This is a surprising commonality for the secondary wives to share with the primary wives. Again, the Deity exercises control over the entirety of the fertility narrative in these two lineages.

While the Deity may be in control, the outcomes are often unpredictable and, at times, seemingly unjust. The Deity's treatment of Leah and Hagar vacillates throughout the account from benevolent at times to dismaying at others. The dubious nature of the Deity toward the women offers no consistent moral architecture with which to accurately predict the responses of the Deity. The Deity does not intervene when Leah and Hagar are treated as pawns in a larger scheme that is devoid of concern for their desires or well-being. The Deity allows Leah to be in a marriage where she is not loved but hated, envied, and overwhelmingly valued less than her sister. Hagar is impregnated without the ability to give consent, is abused by her owner/co-wife, and then commanded to return to the abusive household in a masochistic turn of events (16:9).

Conversely, provisions always seem to be made for the women in their dire circumstances. The Deity saves Hagar and Ishmael's lives twice as they wandered the wilderness, and acts as a guardian every time they are outside of the protection of Abraham's house (16, 21). In Genesis 21:11-13, the narrator shares, "The matter was very distressing to Abraham on account of his son. But God said to Abraham, 'Do not be distressed because of the boy and because of your slave woman...as for the son of the slave woman, I will make a nation of him also, because he is your offspring.'" The text is not specific about which son Abraham is distressed about, but looking at the Deity's response in verse 12, one can infer that Abraham is distressed at Sarah's request to banish Ishmael from his house. Abraham expresses concern over Ishmael, but only the Deity includes Hagar's well-being in the Deity's response to Abraham's protestations. The Deity also acts on Leah's behalf three times, "enabling her to conceive" when it was clear that "[she] was not loved" (29:31, 29:33, 30:17). Although the Deity does not "demonstrate a uniformly affirmative divine judgement"[33] toward Leah and Hagar, the Deity does offer provision of some kind to alleviate their suffering.

The Deity's treatment of Leah and Hagar can be characterized as ambivalence at best, and instrumentalization at worst. The Deity clearly interacts with these two matriarchs in ways that the Deity does not with the primary wives. Leah and Hagar also play significant mother roles in their respective divine lineages, and the Deity takes full advantage of their fecundity to build nations. However, the overarching unpredictable nature of the Deity's relationship to the two women problematizes any accurate prediction of future treatment.

Conclusion

The traditionally diminished reading of Leah and Hagar in the larger biblical narrative belies their substantial contributions to the overall Genesis epic. In reading the two epics together, a number of surprising corollaries materialize. Both the women have difficult relationships with their co-wives who unapologetically see themselves as the primary wife. Leah and Hagar's status as the fertile wife inadvertently generates more hardship than advantage in their polygamous marriages. Both women are reminded of their stature as secondary wives through Abraham and Jacob's treatment. Due to their deleterious place as second-rate wives, their value is diminished in spite of bearing the firstborn son to the patriarch, making them disposable in varying ways. This is yet another example proving that where inequality exists, violence is bred. The Deity is neither the proverbial rescuer nor the perpetrator in these two stories, but something resembling and/both. What cannot be ignored, however, is how involved the Deity is with Leah and Hagar, in ways that are conspicuously absent when it comes to Sarah and Rachel.

Repetition within the Hebrew Bible is always significant and demands a closer examination. The similarities between these two epics are striking and indicate that they should be read together. By doing so, a fuller picture emerges of two complex women in two exceedingly difficult human circumstances with a Deity that is not altogether predictable—not unlike circumstances of modern women. Bach posits an intriguing point, saying, "By rerouting the circuits of conventional comparison, we can clarify and restore the identity to each woman through her relation to an other who embodies and reflects an essential aspect of the female self."[34] An intergenerational conversation ensues which illuminates Leah and Hagar's status within the narrative in ways that are not accomplished when read in a traditional comparison either with their respective co-wives (Leah to Rachel and Hagar to Sarah) or with their lateral social status partner (Leah/Rachel/Sarah and Hagar/Bilhah/Zilpah). By placing Leah and Hagar's lives in conversation with each other across space/time, they serve to empower each other's stories, thereby reclaiming their rightful space in the Genesis family tree.

Notes

1. Alice Bach, ed., *The Pleasure of Her Text: Feminist Readings of Biblical & Historical Texts* (Philadelphia, PA: Trinity Press International, 1990); Norman J. Cohen, "Two That Are One: Sibling Rivalry in Genesis," *Judaism* 32(3), pp. 331–42; Tikva Frymer-Kensky, "Hagar, My Other, My Self," in *Reading the Women of the Bible: A New Interpretation of Their Stories* (New York: Schocken Books, 2002); Bradley C. Gregory, 2008, "The Death and Legacy of Leah in Jubilees," *Journal for the Study of the Pseudepigrapha* 17(2), January, pp. 99–120; Mignon R. Jacobs, *Gender, Power, and Persuasion: The Genesis Narratives and Contemporary Portraits* (Grand Rapids, MI: Baker Academic, 2007); Zvi Jagendorf, 1984, "'In the Morning, Behold, It Was Leah': Genesis and the Reversal of Sexual Knowledge," *Prooftexts* 4(2), pp. 187–92; Nyasha Junior, *Reimagining Hagar: Blackness and Bible* (New York: Oxford University Press, 2019); Elizabeth Wyner Mark, 1998, "The Four Wives of Jacob: Matriarchs Seen and Unseen," *The Reconstructionist* 63(1), pp. 22–35; Jerry Rabow, *The Lost Matriarch: Finding Leah in the Bible and Midrash* (Philadelphia, PA: The Jewish Publication Society, 2014); Tammi J. Schneider, "Hagar," in *Mothers of Promise: Women in the Book of Genesis* (Grand Rapids, MI: Baker Academic, 2008); Phyllis Trible, "Hagar: The Desolation of Rejection," in *Texts of Terror: Literary-Feminist Readings of Biblical Narratives* (London: SCM, 2002).
2. Schneider, "Hagar," 119.
3. In Hebrew, Hagar is a *shiphchah*, which may be translated numerous ways. For more on the translation and usage of the term, see Schneider, 103–5.
4. Sarai/Sarah and Abram/Abraham are used interchangeably throughout the paper, based on their name at the time of the instance referenced.
5. Bernadette Brooten, "Early Christian Women and Their Cultural Context: Issues of Method in Historical Reconstruction," in *Feminist Perspectives on Biblical Scholarship*, ed. Adela Yarbrough Collins, Biblical Scholarship in North America (Chico, CA: Scholars Press, 1985), pp. 65–91.

6. Harold W. Attridge and Wayne A. Meeks, eds., *The Harpercollins Study Bible: New Revised Standard Version, Including the Apocraphal/Deuterocanonical Books with Concordance*, Fully revised and updated; 1st ed (San Francisco: HarperSanFrancisco, 2006).
7. Junior, *Reimagining Hagar*, 2.
8. Polycoity refers to the marriage of a man to an additional, secondary wife who is of a lower social status than the primary wife. See Carol Meyers, Toni Craven, and Ross S. Kraemer, eds., *Women in Scripture: A Dictionary of Named and Unnamed Women in the Hebrew Bible, the Apocryphal/Deuterocanonical Books and the New Testament* (Grand Rapids: Eerdmans, 2002), 170.
9. Trible, "Hagar: The Desolation of Rejection," 11.
10. Jacobs, *Gender, Power, and Persuasion*, 167.
11. Meyers, Craven, and Kraemer, *Women in Scripture*, s.v. "Hagar." See also, Schneider, "Hagar," in *Mothers of Promise*, 117.
12. Meyers et al., *Women in Scripture*, 86.
13. Hagar's attitude towards Sarai and Sarai's responding treatment of Hagar is reflected in Hammurabi law 146, where a slave may claim equality with her owner and the owner may treat her as a common slave.
14. Jacobs, *Gender, Power, and Persuasion*, 172.
15. Samuel A. Berman, *Midrash Tanhuma-Yelammedenu: An English Translation of Genesis and Exodus from the Printed Version of Tanhuma-Yelammedenu with an Introduction, Notes, and Indexes* (Hoboken, NJ: Ktav Publishing House, 1996), Vayetzei 8:3.
16. See Meyers et al., *Women in Scripture*, 86 and Schneider, "Hagar," in *Mothers of Promise*, 117.
17. Jacobs, *Gender, Power, and Persuasion*, 175.
18. Attridge and Meeks, *The Harpercollins Study Bible*, Genesis 29:31–4.
19. Genesis 21:21 shows Hagar as the authoritative chooser of her son's wife. While Rebekah is technically chosen for Abraham's son by a proxy, Abraham is still the ultimate authority behind the decision, as demonstrated in Genesis 24:2–9.
20. Meyers et al., *Women in Scripture*, 170.
21. While this is the case when it comes to their marital relationships, the text never reveals that the children themselves contribute to the women's misery. In fact, it appears that the women have positive relationships with their children and love them (Gen. 30:13, 21:16).
22. William Davidson, "Rashi on Megillah 13b:5:1," The William Davidson Talmud, https://www.sefaria.org/Rashi_on_Megillah.13b.5.1?xml:lang=bi&with=Megillah&lang2=en
23. Jagendorf, "'In the Morning, Behold, It Was Leah,'" 190.
24. Meyers et al., *Women in Scripture*, 170. Economics largely determine the status of a wife in the Hebrew Bible. Meyers et al. elaborate, saying, "Marriage to a primary wife is established on the basis of a conjugal fund property to which both spouses contribute and which becomes the foundation of the economic and legal rights of the primary wife." Since Hagar is Sarai's slave, her economic status clearly delineates her as a secondary wife.
25. Attridge and Meeks, *The Harpercollins Study Bible*, Genesis 16:11.
26. Trible, *Texts of Terror*, 15.

27. At this point in the biblical text, Judaism as it comes to be known has not yet begun; the tradition is amorphous in nature. Hagar presumably would have practiced religious traditions common to her Egyptian heritage.
28. Scott B. Noegel and Brannon M. Wheeler, *The A to Z of Prophets in Islam and Judaism* (Lanham, UK: Scarecrow Press, 2010), p. 154.
29. Schneider, *Mothers of Promise*, 115.
30. Frymer-Kensky, "Hagar, My Other, My Self," 230.
31. Schneider, *Mothers of Promise*, 115.
32. Jagendorf, "'In the Morning, Behold, It Was Leah,'" 189.
33. Rabow, *The Lost Matriarch*, 125.
34. Bach, *The Pleasure of Her Text*. 30.

Works Cited

Attridge, Harold W., and Wayne A. Meeks, eds., 2006, The Harpercollins Study Bible: New Revised Standard Version, Including the Apocraphal/Deuterocanonical Books with Concordance. Fully revised and updated; 1st ed. San Francisco, CA: HarperSanFrancisco.

Bach, Alice, ed., 1990, The Pleasure of Her Text: Feminist Readings of Biblical & Historical Texts, Philadelphia, PA: Trinity Press International.

Berman, Samuel A., 1996, Midrash Tanhuma-Yelammedenu: An English Translation of Genesis and Exodus from the Printed Version of Tanhuma-Yelammedenu with an Introduction, Notes, and Indexes, Hoboken, NJ: Ktav Publishing House.

Brooten, Bernadette, 1985, "Early Christian Women and Their Cultural Context: Issues of Method in Historical Reconstruction," in Adela Yarbrough Collins, ed., Feminist Perspectives on Biblical Scholarship. Biblical Scholarship in North America. Chico, CA: Scholars Press, pp. 65–91.

Cohen, Norman J., 1983, "Two That Are One: Sibling Rivalry in Genesis," Judaism **32**(3), pp. 331–42.

Davidson, William, "Rashi on Megillah 13b:5:1." The William Davidson Talmud. https://www.sefaria.org/Rashi_on_Megillah.13b.5.1?xml:lang=bi&with=Megillah&lang2=en

Frymer-Kensky, Tikva, 2002, "Hagar, My Other, My Self," in Reading the Women of the Bible: A New Interpretation of Their Stories. New York, NY: Schocken Books.

Gossai, Hemchand, 2010, Power and Marginality in the Abraham Narrative, Eugene, OR: Pickwick Publications.

Gregory, Bradley C., 2008, "The Death and Legacy of Leah in Jubilees," Journal for the Study of the Pseudepigrapha **17**(2), January, pp. 99–120.

Jacobs, Mignon R., 2007, Gender, Power, and Persuasion: The Genesis Narratives and Contemporary Portraits, Grand Rapids, MI: Baker Academic.

Jagendorf, Zvi, 1984, "'In the Morning, Behold, It Was Leah': Genesis and the Reversal of Sexual Knowledge," Prooftexts **4**(2), pp. 187–92.

Junior, Nyasha, 2019, Reimagining Hagar: Blackness and Bible, New York: Oxford University Press.

Mark, Elizabeth Wyner, 1998, "The Four Wives of Jacob: Matriarchs Seen and Unseen," The Reconstructionist **63**(1), pp. 22–35.

Meyers, Carol, Toni Craven, and Ross S. Kraemer, eds., 2002, Women in Scripture: A Dictionary of Named and Unnamed Women in the Hebrew Bible, the Apocryphal/Deuterocanonical Books and the New Testament, Grand Rapids, MI: Eerdmans.

Noegel, Scott B., and Brannon M. Wheeler, 2010, The A to Z of Prophets in Islam and Judaism, Lanham, UK: Scarecrow Press.

Rabow, Jerry, 2014, The Lost Matriarch: Finding Leah in the Bible and Midrash, Philadelphia, PA: The Jewish Publication Society.

Schneider, Tammi J., 2008, "Hagar," in Mothers of Promise: Women in the Book of Genesis. Grand Rapids, MI: Baker Academic.

Steinberg, Naomi, 1993, Kinship and Marriage in Genesis: A Household Economics Perspective, Minneapolis, MN: Fortress Press.

Trible, Phyllis, 2002, "Hagar: The Desolation of Rejection," in Texts of Terror: Literary-Feminist Readings of Biblical Narratives, London: SCM.

Yoo, Philip Y., 2016, "Hagar the Egyptian: Wife, Handmaid, and Concubine," The Catholic Biblical Quarterly **78**(2), April, pp. 215–35.

CROSSCURRENTS

QUEER NUNS AND GENDERBENDING SAINTS
Genderf*cking Notions of Normativity

Jessi Knippel

What connections are there between the international queer activist group called the Sisters of Perpetual Indulgence (hereafter the Sisters) and the female saints of the early Christian Church? The bearded yet bedazzled, glittery contemporary queer activists dress as nuns to advocate for "the promulgation of universal joy" and "expiation of stigmatic guilt."[1] Conversely, early Christian female martyrs and saints once donned male dress and assumed male personae as a means to remain faithful and unencumbered by the expectations and obligations of femininity within their cultural context. Certainly, both groups have adopted the dress and aspect of the opposite gender for very different purposes: The drag nuns seek to parody the Church as outsiders, whereas the cross-dressing saints sought to assimilate into it as insiders. But by taking their parody seriously, this paper locates the Sisters within a long lineage of genderbending saints.

This paper builds upon the recent ethnographic research of Melissa Wilcox in her book *Queer Nuns: Religion, Activism and Serious Parody*.[2] It seeks to explore the connections between the Sisters' use of serious parody and their performativity of gender and fruitfully compare it with the historic female saints' presentation of "masculine" identities. How does the performativity of gender in each cultural context challenge and potentially uphold the assumed notions of normative gender? Is it possible to understand the Sisters' actions and presentation as a part of a history of religious "genderf*ck" performativity within the Christian tradition that originated with the genderbending or cross-dressing saints of the early church? Might a similar action be present, for example, in Sister Soami Deluxe's (formerly Sister Missionary Position or Mish) donning a full nun's habit with customary bushy beard, and the fourteenth-century Saint Wilgefortis, with her flowing hair and full, bushy beard?

To engage in this conversation, we will begin with an overview of the Sisters, their history, and the key element of parody that they are incorporating into their activism. From there, we will move into the historical narratives of the genderbending or cross-dressing saints, focusing on the ways in which gender is contextualized in the narratives of Perpetua (d. 202/3 CE), Marinus (Marina) in the fifth (alt. eighth) century, Pelagius (Pelagia) in the fourth to fifth century, and Wilgefortis in the fourteenth century.[3] It will conclude by discussing how the Sisters both live into and counter the tradition of the genderbending saints.

Origins of the Sisters of Perpetual Indulgence

The origin story of the Sisters of Perpetual Indulgence starts on a high holy day filled with boredom. As it has been told both in the history of the order and to Dr. Wilcox, a professor of Religion and Queer/Transgender studies at University of California-Riverside,[4] the first manifestation of the queer nuns was on Holy Saturday of Easter weekend in 1979. Ken Bunch (Sister Adhanarisvara, later renamed Vicious Power Hungry Bitch), Fred Brungard (Sister Missionary Position, later known as Somai), and friend Baruch Golden donned habits with whiteface makeup, props (most notably a toy machine gun), and a camera to document the whole affair. They strolled through San Francisco's Castro neighborhood and on to a nude beach at Lands' End, and finally ended up at a coffee shop in the wealthy Pacific Heights neighborhood.[5] After the reactions the trio received during this impromptu drag session,

> Burch recalls seeing what he termed 'psychological car wrecks' as people gaped at the clearly male nuns, one in makeup holding a toy gun, strolling through the city. 'We realized we had a stick of dynamite,' Burch recalls, 'and that we should do something productive with it. We should use it as a tool for social change, for the change that we want to see.'[6]

This desire to create change led to other manifestations of the Sisters throughout 1979 that included other founding members of the order not present during its first incarnation. Early on The Sisters of Perpetual Indulgence fused religious imagery with performance experiences. These included outsider performance art and dance, drag, and skag drag or genderf*ck. The latter term refers to a version of drag performance that plays with gender cues to purposely challenge or upend normative or conventional notions of gender (e.g., feminine dress, makeup, and hairdos coupled with a beard or visible chest hair).[7]

Recognizing the unsettling power of the image of queer nuns, the Sisters' early parodies of gender and religion furthered their activism and sense of self-agency. By the end of 1979 and into early 1980, the order had been established and became international in scope, with the second official house being the Sydney chapter followed quickly by the first Toronto chapter.[8] Their mission statement articulated their general guiding directive for the "promulgation of universal joy" and "expiation of stigmatic guilt."[9]

Their vibrant physical aesthetic in particular is something of a cross between RuPaul's Drag Race and traditional Catholic habits. Dr. Wilcox describes the Sisters as "people of a wide range of body sizes, shapes and levels of hirsuteness, wearing dresses and white pancake makeup with bright designs and glitter or formal habits with veils cascading down their backs"[10] These outrageous costumes mark the Sisters as something other than traditional Catholic nuns or queer activists. Theirs is a liminal persona that includes elements and aesthetics of the two but is also something else entirely. It is this sense of being "other than" that initially draws attention to the drag nuns and that first caused the "psychological car wrecks" described by Sister Vicious Power Hungry Bitch.[11]

While a version or element of the nun's habit has been a central aesthetic in the Sisters' physical presentation since the beginning, other elements of the persona have varied depending on the house and the Sister. As the order grew and spread nationally and internationally over the next several decades, a few other typical elements developed. Whiteface and drag makeup, sunglasses, and bedazzled and glittered cornets are constant, but at times semi or formal dresses are donned in lieu of traditional habits. The style of habit is generally connected to region or cultural context. Whiteface/drag makeup and various styles of habits and dresses tend to be the normative look for the American and European traditions, whereas the Australian and some English houses favor the combined look of sunglasses and traditional nun's grab without whiteface.[12] Those within the latter tradition feel that the over-the-top drag style of the other houses undermines the "usefulness as a reference to the work of the nuns,"[13] and takes away the clearer reference to religious parody. They maintain that becoming a "parody of a parody"[14] dilutes the message. It becomes a "more recognizable genre of drag than it is a genre of parody of faith and religion."[15]

Sydney's Sister Rowena Keeper of the Holy Doily speaks to it this way, "it is actually a much, much stronger representation, and far, in our opinions, greater parody of foibles and failings of faith, particularly from the organized church view, that it be recognized for what it is by wearing something that is recognizable."[16] Whether in traditional habit and sunglasses or whiteface and evening gown, the presentation of the Sisters is striking and marks the Sisters in the tradition of genderf*ck.

This phenomenon, as described by Wilcox, is a performative construction named as such "because it 'f*cks with' gender: it disrupts taken-for-granted ideas about the predictability of the relationship between gendered traits and appearance, physiological sex, and sexual desire."[17] In regard to the Sisters, this disruption of gender cues is seen in the contrasts between male facial and/or chest hair on the one hand, and the religious habits, dresses, and makeup usually associated with notions of the feminine on the other. To the unaware or uninitiated, the Sisters' religious parody and cross-dressing in habits both challenge and confuse one's assumptions of traditional gender notions and cues. As Wilcox explains,

> The Sisters are working with popular images, the roles implied, and the affect evoked by these tropes or representations that communicate to the people they serve who the Sisters are and what they do. The trope of the nun presents the Sisters as reliable and trustworthy, serious and earnest, engaged in selfless service to those around them. The sharply gendered nature of these imputed qualities is particularly striking.[18]

Dr. Wilcox names their form of parody, "serious parody" because the topsy-turvy spectacle of skag drag causes one to rethink the gendered notions of nuns and their service. Wilcox defines "serious parody" as "a form of cultural protest in which a disempowered group parodies an oppressive cultural institution while simultaneously claiming for itself what it believes to be an equally good or superior enactment of one or more culturally respected aspects of that same institution."[19] For the Sisters, this serious parody presents something beyond dress; it can be found in their commitment to community care, activism, and the veneration and recollection of queer saints.

For example, the Sisters engage in missionary and care work within the LGBTQ community. During this time, often referred to as bar missions,[20] they promote safe sex by passing out care bags and self-created pamphlets. At other times, they offer rituals such as the veil of remembrance and the veil of shame[21] for people to grieve and let go of guilt, respectively. The Sisters' mission is to offer their community absolution from guilt, to assist others in their "right to express their unique joy and beauty,"[22] and to use "humor and irreverent wit to expose the forces of bigotry, complacency and guilt that chain the human spirit."[23]

The Sisters' often advocate for safer sex practices in full nun drag[24] because in certain cases they are more effective than traditional health workers. However, in many houses, there is resistance to engaging in actual sexual activity while wearing the habit.[25] This implies a certain acceptance of the separation of religion and sex.[26] Toward the end of her book, Wilcox reflects on the implications that the order raises around the neoliberal privatization of sex and its separateness from religious imagery, and questions if their activism is contributing to the "biopolitical management of queer bodies" through "state surveillance and control of queer bodies."[27]

By invoking the term "neoliberalism," Wilcox speaks to the ways in which certain pockets of queer communities are able to find acceptance within the dominant culture. For many, the intersections of their queer and religious identities place them permanently outside of the power hierarchies of free-market capitalism, even as they are simultaneously being commodified and consumed for their liminal otherness. At the same time, however, she goes on to note that while the Sisters do have ties to the state and the structure of cultural control and power, their nun work follows a "harm reduction model in which they offer to their communities information and tools but do not dictate behavior or condone and condemn certain actions."[28]

The Sisters' serious parody also can be found in the structure of their membership process, which includes the taking of vows, the taking of a new religious name, and the transformation of the self into one's Sister persona. Naming is common to both traditional religious orders and this queer, specifically drag, culture, and tradition. In each context, as one moves into their public persona—be it drag, queer, or straight nun—they take on a name that represents and embodies their connection to the community and their commitment to the order. Within the Sisters' community, naming can be an individual or communal effort, but it always incorporates wordplay, often with religious and sexualized imagery. Several examples of the more vivid and dynamic of the Sisters' naming style are as follows: Sister Missionary Position,[29] Adhanarisvara/Vicious Power Hungry Bitch/Vish-Knew,[30] Daya Reckoning,[31] Sista Anita Lynchin',[32] Mary Arse Lick and Old Lace[33], Gladness of the Joyous Resuretcum[34], Mysteria of The Holy Order of the Broken Hymen[35], Babylon Anon[36], and Kali Vagilistic X.P. Aladocious.[37]

Over and over within Dr. Wilcox's research, the Sisters talk about the power of their names and clerical personas. Through their naming and activism, the Sisters feel they are engaged in the agency of nun, thereby validating them as nuns. As a result, even as they are spoofing tropes of religious orders and nuns within their cultural context, they are also actually real, self-ordained nuns, acting as nuns act. The reality of their agency as nuns is embodied in the structures and work that they enact within their community contexts. In these ways, it could be said that the Sisters remarkably resemble other religious orders. And yet their sex positivity and stated mission place them outside of the Catholic Christian traditions from which they borrow and build on.

Genderbending Saints

Soon after the beginning of the Jewish movement that was to become the Christian Church, morality tales of exceptional and heroic martyrs and saints floated throughout the community. They upheld communal ideals, offered encouragement to those seeking fortification in their faith, and warned those whose faith was wavering or those who were thinking of leaving the fold. From this hagiographic genre, there emerged several subgenres of narratives that highlighted or touched on gender constructions. Two of these subgenres include elements of genderbending, namely those of the "cross-dressing saint" and the "reformed harlot."

The first subgenre is generally constructed in a threefold plot structure, "(1) flight from the world (2) disguise and seclusion and (3) discovery and recognition."[38] The latter moves from the life of fancy and harlotry, to an encounter with the holy and conversion, to an acetic reconstruction and death. For our purposes, this article looks specifically at elements present in the stories of Perpetua, Marinus (Marina), Pelagius (Pelagia), and Wilgefortis. All these narratives bare elements of the "cross-dressing" category, with St. Pelagia also fitting into the "reformed harlot" trope.

To begin, let us quickly summarize the key narrative points in each story. The first story is that of Perpetua. According to her diary, Perpetua is a young middle-class mother and wife in second-century North Africa, whose conversion to Christianity leads to her condemnation and martyrdom in 202/3 CE. She is jailed along with several other Christians and sentenced to die at the military games in honor of the Emperor. Despite her father's and the magistrates' attempts to change her mind and get her to offer sacrifices to the emperor, Perpetua remains steadfast in her commitment to worship only the Christian God. While in prison awaiting the games in which she will be martyred, Perpetua is given prophetic visions. In one, she turns into a gladiator and bests an Egyptian opponent.

In real life, Perpetua and her fellow companions are finally executed in the games.[39] However, Perpetua's direct and commanding responses to her father and the magistrate, and the genderbending image of her as an embattled gladiator, are unexpected for a woman of her time. For Perpetua, the confusion of her gendering comes across not through physical figure or dress, but rather through her actions, her agency, and her gladiatorial vision.

By contrast, Marinus' (Marina) story, which is alternately set in fifth- or eighth-century Syria, is centered on dress and presentation. After the death of her mother, Marina's father seeks to marry her off before becoming a monk. But Marina does not want to marry and instead joins her father for life in the monastery. To prove her determination, Mary cuts her hair, dresses as a man, and changes her name to Marinus as the pair set off to join a monastic order.

The next ten years goes by with little conflict as the other monks chalk up Marinus' fluid gender cues as the byproducts of the acetic life. But after the death of the father, Marinus is sent from the monastery with two other monks to attend to the community's business, which leads to an overnight stay at an inn. Months later, the innkeeper's daughter falsely accuses Marinus of being the father of her unborn child, as she wishes to protect the identity of her Roman soldier lover. The innkeeper furiously approaches Marinus' abbot, and Marinus is thrown out of the monastery. He sits outside the gates until the innkeeper's grandchild eventually joins Marinus. The two live outside of the monastery for several years until the other monks convince the abbot to reinstate Marinus and the child, provided that Marinus perform the penance of heavy chores.

Marinus dies several years later, his female biological sex is revealed, and all wrongs are righted. Ever since the time Marinus adopts the garb of a monk and changes his name, everything about him aligns with the performance of his perceived gender, including accepting the child he could never have fathered. Marinus is so committed to the perception and performance of "masculinity" that he loses everything (home, life, community) instead of revealing his biological sex.

Our next cross-dressing story is that of Pelagia (Pelagius), a fourth- to fifth-century reformed harlot of sorts who takes on a male persona after her conversion. In the story, Pelagia is a wealthy actress and harlot in Antioch, who converts to Christianity after listening to a sermon by a bishop named Nonnus. While going through the catechism rites for entrance into the faith, the Devil comes trying to collect Pelagia, but Nonnus casts him out, making the sign of the cross and breathing on the old demon. Pelagia subsequently sells all her wealth and releases her slaves. The night before her final entrance into full conversion, Pelagia steals one of Nonnus' tunics (Gk. *chiton*). Disguised as the monk Pelagius, Pelagia heads for a cell she has built on the Mount of Olives and lives out her days as an ascetic monk. For Pelagia, the embrace of a masculine persona offers two forms of freedom. The first is a freedom from the Devil, who leaves the narrative after Pelagia dons the chiton. The second form of freedom is found in her ability to move to live out a solitary life, something seemingly inaccessible to Pelagia if she had stayed in her previous life and if she had stayed within the Christian community. It is also interesting to note that Pelagia presents a form of self-agency and success that is rarely associated with women in these narratives.

The most recent of all the stories is the tale of Wilgefortis[40] which emerges sometime between the eleventh and fourteenth centuries CE. Wilgefortis is the Christian daughter of a pagan Portuguese king and has secretly dedicated her virginity to God. Her father decides to marry her off to a neighboring ruler (the narrative varies as to whether he is a Sicilian pagan or a Portuguese Muslim king). First, she appeals to her father to stop the wedding, yet this only leads to invoking his anger and her being locked in the dungeon. From there, she prays that God will intervene by making her utterly repulsive to the would-be suitor. The next morning her prayers are answered thanks to the appearance of a full lush beard on Wilgefortis' face. This repulses the bridegroom-to-be and further angers her hot-tempered father who demands to know the cause of her changed appearance. When the lady replies that it has come from the God she adores, her father responds in turn by saying, "you shall die, like him you adore," and has his daughter crucified.[41]

The appearance of a non-traditional gender cue such as a beard on a beautiful woman is central to the narrative and acts as both rescue and death sentence for the saint. It is not only off-putting but makes the intended spouse so repulsed that he calls off the wedding. At the same time, however, her appearance and her crucifixion tie her to the person and physicality of Christ. This leads to a blurring (genderf*cking) of the virginal saint Wilgefortis and by extension, inversely, Christ himself.

In all these saints' stories, there is an element of genderbending or cross-dressing, which runs counter to typical or socially constructed norms. Each of these saints uses gender and gender perception as a means of maintaining certain positionality within their faith. Perpetua embraces her masculine persona as a means of fortifying her bout with death. By taking on a prophetic masculine identity, Perpetua is able to not only boldly face the coliseum but is also able to seek the death of a martyr on her own terms and demand the care of her fellow Christians. In the cases of Pelagia and Marinus, the donning of the monk's habit allows them the ability to engage in the monastic life with very little challenge (a least for a while in Marinus' case) because they are no longer bound by the demands of marriage and childbirth that are expected of women in their respective cultures' social structures. And finally for

Wilgefortis, the appearance of a typically male beard becomes the agent of protection for her consecrated virginity and allows for her to die as virgin martyr, holding her faith above her life.

Kristen Upson-Saia analyzes how theses narratives function both in the upholding and stripping of gender perception,

> I argue that these texts received little censure precisely because they worked to strip cross-dressing of its transgressive nature. Through several narrative techniques, these vitae attempted to diffuse the dress practice's challenge to the conventional gender binary by inscribing and naturalizing femininity onto the ascetic's hidden body. Despite this goal, however, [they] paradoxically served to confuse the gender identity of the protagonists. Thus, in the end, the writing of cross-dressing worked for and against notions of a stable gender binary.[42]

As a result, the fluidity of gender (e.g., between Wilgefortis and Christ), and the possible threat of discovery, always leaves the reader with the stark awareness that that the monk is not what they seem.[43] Upson-Saia also speaks to the reader's insider knowledge, as the reader is aware that Marinus is biologically female even as the rest of the characters do not. Once again she says, "Although the disguise is supposed to *conceal* the monk's gender identity, these scenes function to *reveal* to the readers the secondary quality of the saint's masculinity."[44] We the audience consequently become part of the parody of gender being played out in the context of the story.

Even as these stories may seek to strip cross-dressing and gender queering of its power as Upson-Saia suggests, in the end they still open up space for that very action. In their ambiguity of gender and gendered presentation, these narratives of the genderbending or cross-dressing saints create within the Christian tradition a space for narratives that queer normative notions of gender as a binary.

Conclusion: Sisters and Saints Within a Continuing History

The modern genderf*ck of the Sisters of Perpetual Indulgence enters a historical continuum within which gender queering and religion exist in complicated relation. For both the Sisters and the Saints, there is a generative value to assuming a persona that queers and challenges traditional gender cues. In doing so, one speaks to and highlights the reality that gender is more performative than fixed and that it is a construction that is fluid and changing. As Judith Butler says in *Gender Trouble*,

> The parodic repetition of gender exposes as well the illusion of gender identity as an intractable depth and inner substance. As the effects of a subtle and politically enforced performativity, gender is an 'act,' as it were, that is open to splitting, self-parody, self-criticism, and those hyperbolic exhibitions of 'the natural' that, in their very exaggeration, reveal its fundamentally phantasmatic status.[45]

By engaging in the performance of gender that is not expected, both the contemporary activists and the ancient saints challenge and dismantle the notion of gender binary. This in turn offers examples of a cultural space for those who have been marginalized because of their gender presentation.

This opening up of space for gender non-conforming individuals is most needed in the Christian tradition. Locating the Sisters within a long lineage of genderbending saints recovers and updates the Church's history of erasure, which has been intent on eliminating and removing that which it perceives to be transgressive. The Sisters become through their actions "real nuns" by countering this rejection of gender fluidity and by caring for those who are gender fluid through actions of radical acceptance and the expiation of guilt. By engaging in their work as nuns, the Sisters use gender to guard their "holy work," just as the saints used gender queering to guard their sacred faith. It is by challenging gender normativity and affirming gender fluidity in their presentations and performance that The Sisters of Perpetual Indulgence carry on the tradition of the genderbending saints of the early church.

At the same time, however, there are also ways in which each of these traditions can be perceived to be reinforcing problematic notions or constructions of gender even as they are simultaneously challenging them. Even within presentations of gender by the Sisters and saints that challenge normative gender constructions, these normative notions still hold as binaries that are reinforced through communal reactions. For example, within the Wilgefortis narrative, the beard acts as a transgressive gender cue even as it still harkens to the binary. The beard removes any desire for the lady, but she still holds all the other identity markers of an attractive woman. Wilgefortis wants to be rendered repulsive to her would-be husband, but this subliminally tells the audience that no woman with a beard could possibly hold any sense of femininity or attractiveness. In this way, the narrative holds up a binary where women would never have beards lest they become monstrous. Perpetua also presents a narrative that focuses on her direct actions and her embrace of a masculine persona, but her femininity is still highlighted and on display through her body as sexualized object within the text. As Upson-Saia observes, "While early Christian leaders were willing to attribute spiritual 'vitality' to ascetic women, they rarely wished ascetic women to represent such 'manliness' in their dress."[46]

The gender queering of the Sisters and saints acts as a challenge to normative constructions of gender even as it upholds cultural perceptions of gender norms. In the end, there is more that connects these countercultural presentations throughout the ages than separates them. Therefore, through their embodied actions during manifestation of their nun personas within the community and the culture at large, the Sisters challenge and upend traditional notions of gender and religion. So it is that the Sisters stand in direct challenge to conservative religious and cultural notion of a fixed and stable gender binary.

Notes

1. Melissa Wilcox, *Queer Nuns: Religion, Activism, and Serious Parody* (New York: New York University Press, 2018). 66, & "Sistory", 1979, https://www.thesisters.org/sistory
2. Melissa Wilcox, *Queer Nuns: Religion, Activism, and Serious Parody* (New York: New York University Press, 2018).
3. There are no specific dates to be found for the legend of this saint, but we do know that her story comes to popularity in the 14th century.
4. Wilcox Faculty page University of California, Riverside, https://religiousstudies.ucr.edu/full-time-faculty/melissa-m-wilcox/
5. Wilcox, 33.
6. Ibid, 33.
7. Ibid, 32 & https://lgbtrc.usc.edu/files/2015/05/LGBT-Terminology.pdf
8. https://www.thesisters.org/sistory
9. https://www.thesisters.org/sistory
10. Ibid, 3.
11. Ibid, 33.
12. Ibid, 82.
13. Ibid.
14. Ibid.
15. Ibid.
16. Ibid.
17. Ibid, 85.
18. Ibid, 83.

19. Ibid, 70.
20. Ibid, 100.
21. Ibid, 198-201.
22. https://www.thesisters.org/
23. https://www.thesisters.org/
24. Ibid, 100 & 134.
25. Ibid, 207.
26. Ibid.
27. Ibid.
28. Ibid.
29. Ibid, 5.
30. Ibid.
31. Ibid, 134.
32. Ibid, 162.
33. Ibid, 195.
34. Ibid, 63.
35. Ibid, 57.
36. Ibid, 195.
37. Ibid, 23.
38. Davis, Stephen J, *Crossed Text, Crossed Sex: Gender Intertextuality and Gender in Early Christian Legends of Holy Women Disguised as Men*, Journal of Early Christian Studies, pg 7.
39. Rea, Jennifer A. and Clark, Liz, Perpetua's Journey: Faith, Gender, & Power in the Roman Empire.
40. A generic name that is either connected to the latin "virgo fortus" (courageous virgin) or corrupted german "hilgevartz" (holy face) https://historycollection.co/saint-wilgefortis-the-brave-virgin-with-a-beard/
41. https://historycollection.co/saint-wilgefortis-the-brave-virgin-with-a-beard/
42. Upson-Saia, pg 1.
43. Upson-Saia, Kristen, *Gender and Narrative Performance in Early Christian Cross-Dressing Saints' Lives* pg 2.
44. Upson-Saia, pg 2.
45. Butler, Judith, Gender Trouble, 200.
46. Upson-Saia, pg 1.

Works cited

Butler, Judith, 1990, Gender Trouble, New York City, NY: Routledge Press.

Upson-Saia, Kristen, 2010, "Gender and Narrative Performance in Early Christian Cross-Dressing Saints' Lives," Studia Patristica **XLV**, pp. 43–48.

Wilcox, Melissa, 2018, Queer Nuns: Religion, Activism, and Serious Parody, New York City, NY: New York University Press.

Wilgefortis, Saint. https://historycollection.co/saint-wilgefortis-the-brave-virgin-with-a-beard/.

CROSSCURRENTS

NEED WE STILL ASK WHY?
Theodical Futurism and the Sinthomosexual God

Samuel B. Davis

Sinthomosexual -

> Coined by Lee Edelman in his book *No Future: Queer Theory and the Death Drive* (2004), the term refers to either a person or state of being that intentionally takes up a position outside of and opposed to traditional social and moral norms for the purpose of disrupting them.

Introduction

On August 3, 2019, twenty-one-year-old Patrick Crusius entered a Walmart in El Paso, Texas, and opened fire, killing twenty-two people and injuring another twenty-four. Directly after the attack, Crusius drove to a nearby intersection and turned himself into the police, identified himself as the shooter, and admitted to targeting Mexicans.[1] Thirteen hours later, Connor Betts opened fire in downtown Dayton, OH, killing nine people, including his sister, before he was shot to death by local police officers.[2] In this case, at least initially, the shooter left authorities very little clue to his motive, let alone a racially motivated one. In fact, newspapers have pointed out his being a registered democrat[3] and self-proclaimed "leftist" "antifacist."[4]

Mere hours later, Ohio Republican State Representative Candice Keller took to Facebook to share her thoughts on who should take responsibility for such tragedies. "Why not place the blame where it belongs?"

Keller says before providing a long list of reasons why someone would commit such acts of violence. Beginning with the "breakdown of the traditional American family" thanks to transgender folks, same-sex marriage, and "drag queen advocates," she touches on a wide variety of political issues, from kneeling during the national anthem to open borders and lax child discipline, to point out what she sees as a cultural demoralization. To Keller, the "culture" liberals advocate "totally ignores the importance of God and the church," inevitably resulting in mass violence.[5,6,7] There is no denying the political significance of the conversation sparked by Keller. Much of the media discussion since the El Paso shooting, including statements from the majority of Democratic presidential candidates, has been dominated by the question of whether President Donald Trump has encouraged (through rhetoric similar to Keller's) these acts of violence.[8] In an all-to-familiar tone, the El Paso shooter himself states in his manifesto that his views predate Trump and his campaign, using the phrase "fake news" to describe any attempt to blame Trump for the massacre.

In his book, *No Future: Queer Theory and the Death Drive,* Lee Edelman discusses at length the politics of opposition, arguing that the right vs left dualism creates and recreates what he calls "reproductive futurism," the shared goal of an infinitely safe and recognizable future which will always inevitably exclude someone. In identifying this concept, Edelman seeks to address the societal problem of marginalizing that which threatens what Jacques Lacan calls "the symbolic" or "the symbolic order," that which superimposes meaning and morality for any person born within a society. For many, like Candice Keller and Patrick Crusius, the symbolic carries a shared desire for a "native" and "traditionally moral" culture, to which open borders, "drag queen advocacy," same-sex marriage, and a lack of Christian faith are all imminent threats. Edelman's point is that this devotion to an absolute "good" targets and isolates people, often those already pushed to the margin, the most intense examples in this case being Hispanics, Muslims, and the LGBTQ+ community.

Edelman's answer is for the marginalized person ("the Queer") to embrace its societal position. Rather than attempt to blend with the existing culture, Edelman suggests the radical opposite, introducing what he calls, the "Sinthomosexual," the figure who questions the validity of preponderant notions of morality. In order to address the continuing insistence that the only "good" society is a Christian society, this paper takes a close look at the biblical narrative of Job, a story known for its unique style and content.

In this paper, I will be arguing that the book of Job, the poetic book of the Hebrew Bible, provides a space of theological understanding and even sympathy of Edelman's conception of the sinthomosexual in regard to his notion of the "good." Focusing on the theological differences between the prose-style prologue/epilogue with the poetic dialogues, I will discuss the ways the narrative of Job fits within the theoretical framework of Edelman's *No Future*. To do this, I will look primarily at Edelman's discussions of Charles Dickens' *A Christmas Carol* (1843) and Hitchcock's *The Birds* (1963), to demonstrate that the paradoxes in the book of Job provide a useful context for understanding Edelman's greater argument that the moral standards of our society are often upheld at the expense of others.

This paper will begin to discuss the theory of reproductive futurism by demonstrating how it can be understood through what is known as theodicy, or an attempt to understand and explain why a loving God would allow suffering. Taking a moment to closely investigate the details of the book of Job, I will demonstrate that the theological implications of the book of Job are complicated, or perhaps fully realized through the lens of Edelman's *No Future*, reflecting and revealing what I call *theodical futurism*. Ultimately, I argue that the conjunction of Edelman's polemic with that of the story of Job is not only important for understanding meaning broadly, but also relevant theologically and theodically, that is to say, relevant for the understanding of the relationship between human suffering and divine justice, as well as broader societal questions of ethics and morality.

Theodicy and Reproductive Futurism
In his 2008 book, *God's Problem: How the Bible Fails to Answer Our Most Important Question – Why We Suffer*, Bart D. Ehrman begins the chapter "Does Suffering Make Sense?" by detailing an extremely brief history of human suffering both on the micro (namely cancer) and macro (the bubonic plague, the influenza outbreak of 1918, and the current AIDS crisis) levels to discuss the ways the Bible does or does not provide answers to why these sufferings exist.[9] He points out that many public figures, almost

exclusively evangelical Christian men, rely on the Bible as a source of answers and have often rationalized disease epidemics, natural disasters, and horrific events, such as the World Trade Center attacks on September 11, as God dishing out some kind of punishment for our own human wrongdoing. Many of their rationales reference the fate of children either through abortion or lack of conception in the first place, either because of homosexuality, feminist calls for contraception, or other challenges to so-called Christian family values. As the Reverend Jerry Falwell stated on September 13, 2001, while speaking on The 700 Club in direct response to the 9/11 attacks,

> The abortionists have got to bear some burden for [the 9/11 terror attacks] because God will not be mocked. And *when we destroy 40 million little innocent babies,* we make God mad. I really believe *that the pagans, and the abortionists, and the feminists, and the gays and the lesbians* who are actively trying to make that an alternative lifestyle, the ACLU, People for the American Way, all of them who have tried to secularize America, I point the finger in their face and say, "You helped this happen."[10]

A significant percentage of explanations for why God would want to punish an entire city, nation, or the world have pointed to the existence and activity of LGBTQ+ groups and individuals. Zionist Christian Pastor John Hagee famously claimed that Hurricane Katrina was God punishing the city of New Orleans for scheduling a gay pride parade.[11] Pastor Kevin Swanson of the Reformation Church of Elizabeth, Colorado, blamed the devastating 2018 California fires on the state being the first in the United States to legitimize what he called "the sin of homosexuality."[12]

Dr. Ehrman quickly rebukes these interpretations, questioning why God would choose to punish those of the LGBTQ+ community over all others by immediately turning to the suffering of innocent children infected with AIDS "through absolutely no fault of their own." This again invokes the role of the innocent child in searching for theodical answers,

> It is not only homophobic and hateful but also inaccurate and unhelpful to blame [the AIDS] epidemic on sexual preference or promiscuity. Unsafe practices might spread the disease—but why is there a disease in the first place? Are those who suffer the unspeakable emotional and physical agonies of AIDS more sinful and

worthy of punishment than the rest of us? Has God chosen to punish all those AIDS orphans? ... This isn't God who is creating excruciating pain and misery; it certainly isn't something human beings have done to other human beings; and I see nothing redemptive in the *innocent young child* who contracts AIDS, through absolutely no fault of her own, and who can expect nothing but the nightmarish torments that the disease produces.[13]

Ehrman then turns to the book of Job, the story of an innocent man suffering at the hands of God, as a source of explanation for the suffering of "orphans" and "innocent young children," the suffering he gives as proof that there is no reason for suffering, let alone a God-given one.

But there is a complicated politics at work here, a politics thoroughly explored by Lee Edelman in his 2004 book *No Future: Queer Theory and the Death Drive*. In this polemical work, Edelman questions the use of the image of "the Child" as that which perpetuates what he calls "reproductive futurism," a system of societal ordering which casts aside those that would challenge the symbolic order by essentially rejecting the theoretical Child: that which guarantees a continuation of human existence and establishes a moral code, a "structure" of heteronormativity to which all are subject.[14] This heteronormative structure is visibly valorized throughout the Hebrew Bible, when Abraham is assured a progeny as numerous as the stars for upholding the covenant with God.

Within this argument, Edelman places the figure of the "queer" as that which resists and even opposes this social structure, against the rationale of hope and faith in a future, a future from which the queer will always be left or pushed out.[15] Assuming the oppositionality of politics, the queer is posited within this framework as that which paradoxically opposes the logic of opposition itself which defines identity and subjectification, thus refusing "history as linear narrative in which meaning succeeds in revealing itself—*as itself*—through time."[16] Queerness, according to Edelman, is that which destabilizes meaning itself. It calls into question the otherwise unquestionable validity of reproductive futurism, which is strengthened through the continued utilization of the image of the Child and emboldened through the marginalization and demonization of queer folks.

If we apply this theoretical framework to the arguments made by Ehrman, not only does the persistence of reproductive futurism as a stabilizing structure become clear, but his reasoning also begins to fall apart. Although Ehrman is also arguing for a lack of meaning (at least when attempting to understand suffering), by simply mentioning "AIDS orphans" and the "young innocent child who contracted AIDS," he is attempting to generate an immediate reaction on the part of the reader. Ehrman hopes that we will be moved by the image of a sickly child, blameless for its own suffering, begging the question, "why?" while simultaneously providing us an ostensibly comforting answer that "there is no reason." If we are to associate this meaningless suffering with divinity, the only answer is to reject God, for a God that would cause the little children to suffer for seemingly no reason is no God of Ehrman's.[17] But, as Ehrman insists, there are answers to be found within the narrative of Job, so this paper must consider this possibility before connecting Job to the themes of theodicy and the natural reproductive order things.

Job: The Story of Guiltless Suffering

The book of Job is a unique one indeed. Not only is its structure noticeably distinct from other books of the Hebrew Bible, it is also unusually exploratory of differing theological viewpoints.[18]

Structurally speaking, the narrative is built as a series of poetic dialogues, which are framed between a prose folktale prologue and epilogue. In the prologue, the Satan or "the Accuser"[19] comes to God who then brags of his servant Job as being "blameless" and "upright." The Accuser is unsure, arguing that Job is merely obedient because he has been blessed by God and that if God were to take away all he had given him, Job would curse God, ultimately falling from his position of righteousness. Indeed, the author makes it clear that Job is quite blessed in addition to his being upright; at this point in the story, Job has an estimated seven thousand sheep, three thousand camels, five hundred oxen, five hundred donkeys, and many servants, not to mention his three daughters and seven sons, making him the "greatest of all the people of the east."[20] But since the Accuser has presented this challenge to God, God agrees to let Job suffer, and all at once Job's livestock die or are stolen, his servants are all killed, and his children are crushed by a fallen house. The narration makes clear, however, that "in all this Job did not sin or charge God with wrongdoing."[21] But the Accuser is not convinced and argues that if God were to physically harm Job himself, that Job would falter in his blamelessness. God agrees, and Job is then put through horrific pain, covered in sores he has to scrape off his body with a broken piece of pottery. His wife pushes him to "curse God and die" but Job asks, "Shall we receive the good at the hand of God, and not receive the bad?" making clear his retention of integrity. Job's three friends, Eliphaz, Bildad, and Zophar, all come to visit and comfort him, sitting with him in a silence which ends the prologue.[22]

The epilogue, a mere ten verses, continues this folktale style of story, concluding that after all Job's suffering God decides to return all Job had lost twice over, and his seven dead sons and three dead daughters are replaced with brand new ones, and, interestingly enough, Job decides to give the daughters an inheritance alongside their brothers. Job then dies at the ripe old age of 140, having seen the coming of four generations of his lineage.[23]

The rest of the narrative, which are poetic dialogues between Job, his friends, a youth named Elihu, and eventually the divine, make up the vast majority of the book. The prologue and epilogue only take up less than three of the forty-two chapters. Many scholars concur that the dialogues noticeably differ from the prologue and epilogue in terms of the style, theology, and language, and they suggest that these were written by different authors at different times. For example, Job's character is noticeably depicted as humble and penitent in the prose narrative at the beginning and end of the book. "Naked I came from my mother's womb, and naked shall I return there; the Lord gave, and the Lord has taken away; blessed be the name of the Lord."[24] But within the dialogues, Job is full of complaints: "Let the day perish when I was born...Why did I not die at birth, come forth from the womb and expire?...I will speak in the anguish of my spirit; I will complain in the bitterness of my soul."[25]

The Book of Job has been formed over time into its current whole through consolidation of these different narrative threads. This helps to explain a few discrepancies and contradictions within the narrative, one of which is central to my argument: the theological differences in understandings of suffering and divine punishment. Specifically, on the one hand, there is the linear narrative of the prologue and epilogue, where Job's unfailing faith is tested, found worthy, and rewarded. This suggests that God rewards and punishes humans on the basis of merit. Job passed the test of God's will. On the other hand, however, there is the continuing theme throughout the poetic dialogues—the back and forth conversations between Job and his friends Eliphaz, Bildad, and Zophar, and Job's confrontation with God—which suggests a very different story. It is this story that will provide the narrative's harmonization with Edelman's discussion of queerness and destabilization of the notion of the "good," which is premised on reproductive futurism.

Theodical Futurism and the Sinthomosexual God

Job's three friends present to Job what they see as the only commonsensical explanations for Job's suffering from within the context of their stable world order, beginning with Eliphaz: "Think now, who that was innocent ever perished? Or where were the upright cut off? As I have seen, those who plow iniquity and sow trouble reap the same…Their Children are far from safety, they are crushed in the gate, and there is no one to deliver them."[26] Bildad asks similar questions: "Does God pervert justice? Or does the Almighty pervert the right? If you will seek God and make supplication to the Almighty, if you are pure and upright, surely then he will rouse himself for you and restore to you your rightful place."[27] Then, Zophar offers his answer: "Know that God exacts of you less than your guilt deserves…For he knows those who are worthless; when he sees iniquity will he not consider it?"[28] The three friends of Job here take as assumption that Job's suffering is due to some wrong he or his children have committed, that God would not punish him if this were not the case, for within their theological worldview God rewards the faithful and punishes the wicked.

Considering for a moment that Job's friends are correct, as this would effectively make sense of the events of the prose narrative, what would this mean of God's will, given his full awareness and insistence that "[Job] still persists in his integrity, although you incited me against him, to destroy him *for no reason*?"[29]

While reading Edelman, the senseless suffering of Job, and the emotional impact it elicits in the reader, initially recalls the character of Tiny Tim in Charles Dickens' *A Christmas Carol*. Edelman writes,

His 'withered little hand' as if in life already dead, keeping us all in a stranglehold as adamant as the 'iron frame' supporting his 'little limbs'; his 'plaintive little voice' refusing any and every complaint the better to assume its all-pervasive media magnification, in the echoes of which, year in and year out, God blasts us, every one; his 'little, little' figure parading its patent vulnerability with the all-too-sure conviction of embodying the ruthless spiritual uplift, the obligatory hope for the future to come.[30]

Quickly one might notice a bit of a connection between Tiny Tim and Job, whose vulnerability is also graphically described throughout the narrative in a similarly "plaintive" fashion. "My flesh is clothed with worms and dirt, my skin hardens, then breaks out again"; but it is within the friends so-called comfort of Job which we find this "ruthless spiritual uplift" Edelman is critical of: "He will yet fill your mouth with laughter, and your lips with shouts of joy."[31] It is through Job's friends in which the reader is comforted in the redemption of Job and in the end can find some kind of "hope" in a possible future. But, like Edelman, Job is not at all satisfied with this answer:

> If it is a matter of justice, who can summon [God]? Though I am innocent, my own mouth would condemn me; though I am blameless, he would prove me perverse. I am blameless; I do not know myself; I loathe my life. It is all one; therefore I say, he destroys both the blameless and the wicked. When disaster brings sudden death, he mocks at the calamity of the innocent. The earth is given into the hand of the wicked; he covers the eyes of its judges – if it is not he, who then is it? I will say to God, do not condemn me; let me know why you contend against me. Does it seem good to you to oppress, to despise the work of your hands and favor the schemes of the wicked?[32]

Speaking to what Edelman calls a "truly hopeless wager," that is, "attending to the persistence of something internal to reason that reason refuses...deliberately sever[ing] us from ourselves, from the assurance, that is, of knowing ourselves and hence of knowing our 'good',"[33] Job demands an explanation he knows he may never receive, much less understand. Unlike his friends, but like Edelman, Job attempts to call out what he sees as a meaninglessness in the world order (the Lacanianpsychoanalytic symbolic order), a fruitlessness in attempting to find solace in a morality one can never hope to fully understand as anything other than an unjust, unbalanced system which protects the strong and preys on the weak and vulnerable.

As Edelman points out, "*A Christmas Carol* would have us believe we know whom to blame already, know as surely as we know who would silence the note of that plaintive little voice," and immediately, we are struck by the image of the scowling, angry, cold, child-hating Ebenezer Scrooge.[34]

Scrooge, for Edelman, signifies what he calls, the "Sinthomosexual," the figure that rejects futurity, asserting itself as that which stands against the idea of a future at all by existing as the very antithesis to the fiction of stability in reality. Edelman, a trained literary critic, paints Scrooge as the queer who stands up against the image of the Child, and by extension reproductive futurism. He assumes a stance which actively denies Tiny Tim a future, for no reason other than his own enjoyment, an "enjoyment alien to that of the community at large, and alien, more importantly, to the very concept of community at all."[35]

At the very same moment, however, Edelman reminds us (without explicitly naming) who is *actually* to blame for this "dreaded pedocide."[36] He suggests that perhaps when we see the crippled Tiny Tim at the church, we aren't at all reminded of "who made lame beggars walk, and blind men see," but rather "who made the lame beggars lame (and beggars) and who made those blind men blind"[37] in the first place. Bart Ehrman brings up this very issue to ask,

> Why? Many readers have taken comfort in the circumstance that once Job passed the test, God rewarded him. But what about Job's children? Why were they *senselessly* slaughtered? So that God could prove a point? Does this mean that God is willing—even eager—to take *my* children in order to see how I'll react? Possibly the most offensive part of the book of Job is at the end, when God restores all that Job had lost—including additional children. Job lost seven sons and three daughters and, as a reward for his faithfulness, God gives him an additional seven sons and three daughters. What was this author thinking? That the pain of a child's death will be removed by the birth of another? What kind of God is this? Do we

> think that everything would be made right if the six million Jews killed in the Holocaust were 'replaced' by six million additional Jews born in the next generation? As *satisfying* as the book of Job has been to people over the ages, I have to say I find it supremely *dissatisfying*. If God tortures, maims, and murders people just to see how they will react—to see if they will not blame him, when in fact he is to blame—then this does not seem to me to be a God worthy of worship. Worthy of fear, yes. Of praise, no.[38]

In response to Ehrman's dissatisfaction, Edelman's polemic shows us that the comfort people feel for the redemption Job receives is a satisfaction not of the replacement of lost property, or even of lost children, but a regaining of a lost future. I would argue further that the satisfaction Ehrman is looking for is what I would call *theodical futurism*: an insistence that a just God, a God that is worthy of worship, must be able to answer for the death of the innocent Child. This God must somehow justify the child who suffers for no reason, and whose suffering is solely the responsibility and will of God alone.

From the perspective of *No Future* (what I would argue is the perspective of Job as well), the ending of the book of Job is no more or less satisfying than that of the ending of *A Christmas Carol*. These endings are designed to "preserve the fantasy" of reproductive futurism (or theodical futurism in the case of Job), granting reprieve to the sinthomosexual Scrooge insofar as he is willing to reject himself, providing the readers a security of their own future by becoming "a second father" to Tiny Tim.[39]

In the case of Job, it is only after God gives Job "twice as much as he had before" that his "brothers and sisters and all who had known him before"—those who had "failed" him, "forgotten" him, "abhor[red]" him, and "estranged" themselves from him during his undeserved torment—come to him to show him sympathy and comfort "for all the evil that the Lord had brought upon him."[40] It is only once they recognize that God himself had committed this evil, a recognition I stress is only gained *through* God's restoration of Job, that they are willing to provide company and comfort.

I would be surprised if the dissatisfaction felt by Ehrman, as well as the positionality and importance of *No Future*, weren't also felt by Job himself. As I will discuss in the next section, Job ultimately receives no actual answer from God explaining why this suffering occurred, and it is in fact God, not Job, whose evil begs redemption in the end. Thus, if there is any sinthomosexual within the narrative of Job, it is God himself, through his lack of keeping to any clear moral code and challenging Elihu's all-to-sure moral conviction that Job suffered *because he deserved it*. Furthermore, the theodical significance of the book of Job, particularly for the task laid out in *No Future*, lies not in its attempt at an explanation of human suffering, but rather in its insistence that suffering is in fact meaningless.

Authority, Opposition, and the Queer Irony of the Sinthomosexual

I have already touched on the poetic dialogues between Job and his so-called friends above, in which they persist in their accusations that Job, or his children, must have done something wrong to anger God. They continually insist that God does not punish the righteous and only punishes the wicked, but Job is more than convinced of his own righteousness and consistently rebukes their charges, opposing their theological moral claims by declaring what he sees as obvious injustice:

> Why do the wicked live on, reach old age, and grow mighty in power? Their children are established in their presence, and their offspring before their eyes. Their houses are safe from fear, and no rod of God is upon them. Their bull breeds without fail; their cow calves and never miscarries. They send out their little ones like a flock, and their children dance around. They sing to the tambourine and the lyre and rejoice to the sound of the pipe. They spend their days in prosperity, and in peace they go down to Sheol.[41]

Ehrman suggests this injustice might be less repugnant if there was some notion that the innocent and faithful would be rewarded in some afterlife while the wicked finally received their proper punishment, but as with most books of the Hebrew Bible, there is none.[42] But again, Ehrman's comment makes clear this desire of his, and likely many others, for this theodical futurism, in which God can provide some explanation for his allowing of such injustice. But, as I mentioned above, and will show below, God provides no answer for Job regarding justice at all.

Throughout the poetic dialogues, Job regularly asks that God give him an audience that he might defend himself against God, but it is only in his final speech in which his words seem to reach God, as this is Job's final statement before being confronted by God:

> O that I had one to hear me! (Here is my signature! Let the Almighty answer me!) O that I had the indictment written by my adversary! Surely I would carry it on my shoulder; I would bind it on me like a crown; I would give him an account of all my steps; like a prince I would approach him."[43]

Following these final words of Job's, after which his three friends had given up on convincing Job of his guilt, a fourth and final figure, unmentioned before his speech, decides to share his thoughts on the matter. Elihu, the youngest of the crowd, had apparently been waiting to speak out of respect for his elders, but at this point he expresses that his anger won't allow him to stay silent any longer. He begins the longest speech of the entire book by rebuking the other friends for not saying anything to refute Job's statements. He claims to be speaking in defense of God, then proceeds to say little the others hadn't already said before. Scholars agree,[44] partly because he goes unmentioned anywhere else in the book, that Elihu's speech was a later addition to the narrative. As such, there are some points that are worth noting.

After essentially accusing Job of blasphemy for focusing on his own righteousness rather than the righteousness of God, Elihu makes several statements that help clarify God's later response to Job. First, Elihu calls upon the other wise men to join him in his accusations of Job, "Hear my words, you wise men, and give ear to me, you who know; for the ear tests words and the palate tastes food. Let us choose what is right; let us determine among ourselves what is good."[45] This statement is intriguing, particularly after his admission that he was young in years, as he comes across rather confidently that he knows, or at least can determine, what is essentially "right" and "good." He positions himself as God's defender, as a seemingly last-ditch effort to teach Job some kind of lesson he has not yet learned: "Therefore, hear me, you who have sense, far be it from God that he should do wickedness, and from the Almighty that he should do wrong. For according to their deeds he will repay them, and according to their ways he will make it befall them."[46] Appearing yet again is this position that God is just and judges solely based on merit, adding for effect the suggestion that anyone with "sense" would accept this position.

Going even further, Elihu then claims to speak for God himself, "Bear with me a little, and I will show you, for I have yet something to say on God's behalf. I will bring my knowledge from far away and ascribe righteousness to my Maker. For truly my words are not false; one who is perfect in knowledge is with you."[47] Whether Elihu is referring to God or himself as "one who is perfect in knowledge" is unclear, but what is clear is Elihu's belief that he is speaking only truth, and that God's justice is absolute and unquestionable. In this certainty of the natural order of things, are we not reminded of Edelman's "*all-too-sure conviction* of embodying the ruthless spiritual uplift, the obligatory hope for the future to come?"[48] And by contrast, should we not recall what Edelman also suggests as the desired positionality of queerness, a queerness that would "sever us from ourselves, from the assurance, that is, of knowing ourselves and hence of knowing our 'good?'"[49]

From Elihu's self-assured statements, we can begin to understand his role in the symbolic order of theodical futurism. From this perspective, Elihu can be seen as the epitome of heteronormativity constructed within the social order, relying completely on the stability of his own sense of moral reality which he so desperately holds on to as absolute truth. But as Edelman shows us, any absolute notions of "truth" and "reality" are anything but stable, and as we begin to unpack God's refusal to answer to Job's questions of divine justice, Elihu's harsh criticisms and accusations of blasphemy ring utterly hollow. In this context, the sinthomosexuality of God becomes increasingly plausible.

The rest of Elihu's speech seems to serve as a kind of introduction for God's grand entrance. This introduction alludes to God's righteousness and sense of justice, but its principal function is to intimidate Job and to underscore God's sheer power, authority, and dominance over puny humanity. Elihu declares, for example,

> Listen, listen to the thunder of his voice and the rumbling that comes from his mouth; God thunders wondrously with his voice; he does great things that we cannot comprehend; From its chamber comes the whirlwind, and cold from the scattering winds; The

> Almighty – we cannot find him; he is great in power and justice, and abundant righteousness he will not violate.[50]

Leaving us with this bold final statement reasserting God's righteousness, it is in this moment in which God suddenly appears before Job. After this, there is no longer any mention of Elihu, and Job's friends don't appear again until the epilogue, which suggests an intimate encounter between Job and God.

However intimate, the encounter can only be interpreted as terrifying. God appears to Job not as a voice calling from above, nor as any earthly being, but as a whirlwind, or better understood as a storm or tornado, assuming the presence of lightning, thunder, and a strong wind coming from heavenly chambers. God then begins his series of speeches directed toward Job, which primarily take the form of unanswerable questions, clearly mocking Job's complaints and claims of defensibility:

> Who is this that darkens counsel by words without knowledge? Gird up your loins like a man, I will question you, and you shall declare to me. Where were you when I laid the foundation of the earth? Tell me, if you have understanding. Who determined its measurements – surely you know! Or who stretched the line upon it? On what were its bases sunk, or who laid its cornerstone when the morning stars sang together and all the heavenly beings shouted for joy? Have you entered into the springs of the sea, or walked in the recesses of the deep? Have the gates of death been revealed to you, or have you seen the gates of deep darkness? Have you comprehended the expanse of the earth? Declare if you know all this. Shall a faultfinder contend with the Almighty? Anyone who argues with God must respond.[51]

Instead of responding to Job's complaints, God dismisses them by simply resorting to his position of authority. His defense is a more than satisfactory offense. He asserts his superiority, belittles Job, and invalidates Job's right to even question his creator and knower of all things. God's power play has its intended effect. Considering the fact that these questions possess no possible answer, Job's response is again reminiscent of Tiny Tim's "plaintive" manner. "See, I am of small account; what shall I answer you? I lay my hand on my mouth. I have spoken once, and I will not answer twice, but will proceed no further."[52] Job is presumably awe-struck, but offers no definite capitulation, instead deferring any further response until the very end. God's response is again calling for Job to gird up his loins like a man, a phrase meant to suggest a kind of battle for which Job must be prepared, before asking the question, "Will you even put me in the wrong? Will you condemn me that you may be justified?"[53] As perhaps the only time this happens, God seems to acknowledge his understanding of what Job has been asking for, which is an explanation of what Job sees as injustice for which he believes God should have to answer.

But God doesn't answer Job's critique, and instead, *ironically* tells him to take up the task himself of ridding the world of that which Job finds deplorable:

> Deck yourself with majesty and dignity; clothe yourself with glory and splendor. Pour out the overflowings of your anger and look on all who are proud, and abase them. Look on all who are proud and bring them low; tread down the wicked where they stand. Hide them all in the dust together; bind their faces in the world below. Then I will acknowledge to you that your own right hand can give you victory."[54]

Like Edelman's *No Future*, God is suggesting an impossible task (and an ironic task at that): the reordering of meaning with the promise of gaining virtually nothing. But most significantly, God (or rather the Biblical author) presents this irony as the closest Job is going to get to a satisfactory answer to his demands.

For Edelman, through his reading of Paul de Man's *Aesthetic Ideology* (1996), irony serves as the literary challenge to the ostensible reality that narrative attempts to stabilize.[55] If narrative is the logic with which meaning is figured linearly, irony, as "syntactical violence," is that which reveals and disrupts the fantasy of sensical linear signification and identity formation, albeit "inextricable from the articulation of narrative as such."[56] Inextricable from the narrative of the book of Job, the irony that God poses challenges any and all conceptions of "right," "wrong," "truth," or "good" within said narrative, to the dissatisfaction of anyone devoted to theological propriety. The mocking which Job endures seems tantamount to a grade schooler being lectured by a scornful teacher: "Where were you when I laid the foundation of the earth? Tell me, if you have understanding. Who determined its measurements—surely you know!" This ultimately renders Job virtually speechless, devoid of any sense of opposition: "I know that you can do all things, and that no purpose of yours can be thwarted. Therefore I have uttered what I did not understand, things too wonderful for me, which I did not know. I had heard of you by the hearing of the ear, but now my eye sees you; therefore I despise (submit) myself and repent (am comforted) in dust and ashes."[57] Not only this, but God appears to *enjoy* this whole process, an appearance of excitement that suggests God's own kind of *jouissance*, excess, or death drive: that which drives the sinthomosexual's rejection of that which claims to provide moral meaning.

The sinthomosexual figure of God in the book of Job does theologically what Edelman proposes politically. Edelman's proposition is for queerness to accept and embrace its own negativity, the value for which lies in its challenge to the value of the social itself. For if queer theory's efficacy, as Edelman argues, lies in opposing oppositionality itself,[58] then politically this means taking up a position not only outside of but oppositional to a politics built on opposition. If oppositional politics determines and reproduces the governing fantasy of reproductive futurism,[59] the "side" the queer must take is the side that questions any absolute notion of an inherent "good" in the logic of reproductive futurism. This is a "good" that every political platform accepts unquestioningly. This is because questioning this "good" would question the narrative realization of a future worth striving for.[60] Ohio State Representative Candice Keller makes the case that Obama, homosexuals, and leftist liberal culture are to blame for domestic mass shootings because they ignore the importance of God and the church. However, mass murderers like the ones in Poway, CA, and Christchurch, New Zealand, base much of their justification on Biblical scripture. This is an inherent opposition that keeps politics polarized. Ultimately, the fact that there are people, such as the El Paso gunman, who believe there is an inherent "good" in killing as many people as possible to protect a supposed culture from moral degradation, is a problem that may never be addressed.

Looking back at the story of Job, the theology found within both the prose narrative and poetic dialogues is unequivocally oppositional. The story begins with the Satan, also called the Accuser, challenging the notion that the blameless Job could be righteous for any reason other than his expectation of a reward. Thus begins the test. Job's suffering is then never free of opposition, his friends questioning every single response Job has. They can't understand a notion of suffering that doesn't involve an oppositional theology in which there is always a notion of an absolute "good" that is divinely and justly governed. God, however, completely rejects, opposes, even scoffs at the notion of an oppositional theology that justifies itself based on false propriety, on the fantasy of a God concerned with human justice made real by theodical futurism. Job's constant inquiry of "why?" is swiftly silenced by God's uniquely non-sensical, even fantastical explanation that there is no reason. By effectively saying "That's just the way it is," the book of Job itself queers the presupposed order of things. There is no *nomos*; all is anomaly.

"Need We Still Ask Why?"

In the final chapter of *No Future,* Edelman formulates the figure of the sinthomosexual with that of the murderous birds in Alfred Hitchcock's *The Birds* (1963). Intriguingly, Edelman emphasizes the meaninglessness embraced, or rather championed, by the sinthomosexual figure by capturing the enigmatic draw of Hitchcock's film. Curious film goers, critics, and even characters within the film asked "What do the bird attacks mean?"[61]

> What do the bird attacks mean? 'What do you suppose made it do *that*?' wonders Melanie Daniels after the first gull gashes her head. 'What's the matter with *all* the birds?' asks Lydia Brenner following a full-scale assault on the children celebrating her daughter's eleventh birthday. 'Why are they doing this, the birds?' young Cathy inquires of her older brother, Mitch, echoing the question that an overwrought mother poses to Melanie in the wake of an attack on the center of Bodega Bay: 'Why are they doing this? Why are they *doing* this?' But why, we might ask, need we still ask why?[62]

In response to the series of questions posed by the characters, Edelman asks the poignant question this paper also rhetorically poses: "But why, might we ask, need we still ask why?"[63] For Edelman, the clear purpose of the pedocidical birds is argued most persuasively by Robin Wood as "the possibility that life is meaningless and absurd."[64] For many, the equally pedocidical God of the book of Job suggests nothing more than the same possibility.

For Bart Ehrman, however, this explanation is not good enough:

> Does the fact that he's almighty give him the right to torment innocent souls and murder children? Does might make right? Moreover, if the point is that we cannot judge the cruel acts of God by human standards, where does that leave us? In the Bible, aren't humans made in the image of God? Aren't human standards given by God? Doesn't he establish what is right and fair and just? Aren't we to be like him in how we treat others? If we don't understand God by human standards (which he himself has given), how can we understand him at all, since we're human? Isn't this explanation of God's justice, at the end of the day, simply a cop-out, a refusal to think hard about the disasters and evils in the world as having any meaning whatsoever?[65]

Given the discussion formulated throughout this paper, I am quick to question what exactly Ehrman is looking for in Job. The dissatisfaction he expresses in Job's "redemption" seems now to miss much of the point. Does the book not seem to question the very notion of a "right" at all? Is it not made clear that "human standards" of what is "right and fair and just" are not necessarily concerns of God? Or at least, that they take on a different meaning? Is it really a simple cop-out for a theological manuscript to question the very notion of meaning?

I turn once more to Edelman for what would likely be his response to Ehrman: "Rather than expanding the reach of the human, we might insist on enlarging the *inhuman* instead—or enlarging what, in its excess, in its unintelligibility, exposes the human itself as always misrecognized catachresis, a positing blind to the willful violence that marks its imposition."[66]

The narrative of Job undeniably argues that there is an irreconcilable gap between God and humanity, a gap which God himself spends considerable time making clear to Job by way of endless boasting of his "comprehension of the expanse of the earth" and ability to "draw out Leviathan with a fishhook."[67] In the end, God speaks to Job's three friends, telling them "you have not spoken of me what is right, as my servant Job has," a final gesture on the part of God that, although still provides no answer to Job's demands, squashes the theodical futurism these three friends held onto so tightly and which tormented an already unfairly tormented Job. Additionally, if we recall correctly, the story's ending includes a rebuke of God, which makes clear the "evil that the Lord had brought upon [Job]."[68] Despite the story's reimbursement-like resolution, the reader is reminded to be aware that the God of Job is not a just ruler as Elihu so vociferously proclaims. The reckless assumption to know what is right or just blinds Elihu and his many allies to the suffering Job endures; a suffering not due to his or anyone else's sin, but to an unwarranted accusation of *potential* infidelity.

Perhaps, as realized through the frame of *No Future*, the resolution of Job is not meant to be a resolution at all, but rather an uncomfortable and unsatisfyingly brief end to the queerest story in the Bible. This is a story that, if taken seriously, could call into question much, if not most of the religious rationales that rely on the Bible to determine morality and judgment. In the end, Job (or rather the author) seems to understand better than most the potential absurdity of social order, as Job's three daughters are not only given names—Jemimah, Keziah, and Keren-happuch—a rare occurrence in the Hebrew Bible, but it is also noted that they are provided an inheritance alongside their male siblings, which the New Oxford Annotated Bible notes as simply "an unusual practice."[69]

In this increasingly polar and hostile political environment, Job and Edelman provide important reminders that judgment is often nothing more than assumption, an adoption of cultural values that are superimposed on anyone born within our society and maintained through the discrimination and marginalization of vulnerable peoples.

Notes
1. Cedar Attanasio, Jake Bleiberg, and Paul J. Weber, *Police: El Paso Shooting Suspect Said He Targeted Mexicans*, ABC News (2019).
2. Kevin Williams et al., "Gunman Killed Sister, Eight Others in Second Deadly U.S. Mass Shooting in 24 Hours," *The Washington Post* (August 4 2019), accessed August 10, 2019, https://www.washingtonpost.com/nation/2019/08/04/nine-fatally-shot-dayton-including-suspect-day-after-mass-shooting-texas/.
3. Jennifer Doherty, "Who Is Connor Betts? Dayton Shooting Suspect Identified by Police," *Newsweek* (August 4 2019), accessed August 10, https://www.newsweek.com/who-connor-betts-dayton-ohio-shooter-1452491.

4. Paul P. Murphy et al., "Dayton Shooter Had an Obsession with Violence and Mass Shootings, Police Say," *CNN* (August 7 2019), accessed August 10, 2019, https://www.cnn.com/2019/08/05/us/connor-betts-dayton-shooting-profile/index.html.
5. Alex Horton, "Ohio Republican Blames Mass Shootings on 'Drag Queen Advocates,' Colin Kaepernick and Obama," *The Washington Post* (August 5 2019), accessed August 10, 2019, https://www.washingtonpost.com/politics/2019/08/05/ohio-republican-blames-mass-shootings-drag-queen-advocates-colin-kaepernick-obama/?noredirect=on.
6. Interestingly, while many are quick to point out the harm in blaming those who are the targets of violence, not a single news article on Keller's words mentions her concern for the importance of God and the church, or anti-Semitism.
7. Keller's rhetoric, although dubbed abhorrent, is not off base. On the contrary, she won her senate seat as an extreme conservative, echoing much of President Donald Trump's campaign rhetoric. Even when disregarding nativism, the morals she champions are highly political and ring strongly with Christian evangelicals.
8. Philip Rucker, "'How Do You Stop These People?': Trump's Anti-Immigrant Rhetoric Looms over El Paso Massacre," *The Washington Post* (August 4 2019), accessed August 10, 2019, https://www.washingtonpost.com/politics/how-do-you-stop-these-people-trumps-anti-immigrant-rhetoric-looms-over-el-paso-massacre/2019/08/04/62d0435a-b6ce-11e9-a091-6a96e67d9cce_story.html.
9. Bart D. Ehrman, *God's Problem : How the Bible Fails to Answer Our Most Important Question-- Why We Suffer*, 1st ed. (New York: HarperOne, 2008), 162. Italics my own.
10. Goodstein, Laurie. "Falwell: Blame Abortionists, Feminists and Gays." The Guardian. Guardian News and Media, September 19, 2001. https://www.theguardian.com/world/2001/sep/19/september11.usa9.
11. *Pastor John Hagee on Christian Zionism*, directed by Terry Gross (NPR, 2006), https://www.npr.org/templates/story/story.php?storyId=6097362?storyId=6097362.
12. Curtis M. Wong, "Pastor Blames California Wildfires on State's Embrace of Lgbtq Rights," *Huffington Post* (August 6 2018), https://www.huffingtonpost.com/entry/kevin-swanson-california-wildfires_us_5b68552ae4b0de86f4a391ae.
13. Bart D. Ehrman, *God's Problem: How the Bible Fails to Answer Our Most Important Question – Why We Suffer*, 164.
14. Lee Edelman, *No Future : Queer Theory and the Death Drive*, Series Q (Durham: Duke University Press, 2004), 2-3.
15. Ibid., 3.
16. Ibid., 4.
17. Ehrman, 162.
18. Michael David Coogan et al., *The New Oxford Annotated Bible with the Apocryphal/Deuterocanonical Books : New Revised Standard Version*, Augm. 3rd ed. (Oxford ; New York: Oxford University Press, 2007), 726.
19. To be distinguished from the later "devil" who becomes known as the adversary of God. Here "the Satan" is one of God's heavenly beings, the one who travels about the Earth accusing humans of wrongdoing.
20. Job 1:1-5
21. Job 1:13-22

22. Job 2
23. Job 42:7-17
24. Job 1:21
25. Job 3:3, 11; 7:11
26. Job 4:7-8; 5:4
27. Job 8:3, 5-6
28. Job 11:6, 11
29. Job 2:3
30. Edelman, 41-42.
31. Job 8:21
32. Job 9:19-24
33. Edelman, 5.
34. Ibid., 42.
35. Ibid., 43.
36. Ibid.
37. Edelman.
38. Ehrman, 171-72.
39. Edelman, 47.
40. Job 42:11
41. Job 21:7-13
42. Ehrman, 181.
43. Job 31:35-37
44. Michael David Coogan, Marc Zvi Brettler, and Carol A. Newsom, *The New Oxford Annotated Bible*, College ed. (Oxford: Oxford University Press, 2007), 758.
45. Job 34:2-4
46. Job 34:10-11
47. Job 36:1-4
48. See note 20.
49. Edelman, 5.
50. Job 37:2, 5, 9, 23
51. Job 38:2-7, 16-18; 40:2
52. Job 40:5-6
53. Job 40:8
54. Job 40:10-14
55. Edelman, 23-24.
56. Ibid., 24.
57. Job 42:2-6
58. Edelman, 24.
59. Ibid., 17.
60. Ibid., 7.
61. Ibid., 119.
62. Ibid.
63. Edelman, 119.
64. Ibid., 120.

65. Ehrman, 188-89.
66. Edelman, 152.
67. Job 38:18; 41:1
68. Job 42:11
69. Coogan, Brettler, and Newsom, 771.

Work Cited

Attanasio, Cedar, Jake Bleiberg, and Paul J. Weber, 2019, Police: El Paso Shooting Suspect Said He Targeted Mexicans, ABC News.

Coogan, Michael David, Marc Zvi Brettler, and Carol A. Newsom, 2007a, The New Oxford Annotated Bible, College ed., Oxford: Oxford University Press.

Coogan, Michael David, Marc Zvi Brettler, Carol A. Newsom, and Pheme Perkins, 2007b, The New Oxford Annotated Bible with the Apocryphal/Deuterocanonical Books: New Revised Standard Version, Augm. 3rd ed, Oxford; New York: Oxford University Press.

Doherty, Jennifer,2019, "Who Is Connor Betts? Dayton Shooting Suspect Identified by Police," Newsweek. Accessed August 10. https://www.newsweek.com/who-connor-betts-dayton-ohio-shooter-1452491.

Edelman, Lee, 2004, No Future: Queer Theory and the Death Drive, Series Q, Durham: Duke University Press.

Ehrman, Bart D., 2008, God's Problem: How the Bible Fails to Answer Our Most Important Question-Why We Suffer, 1st ed, New York, NY: HarperOne.

Pastor John Hagee on Christian Zionism. Directed by Gross, Terry. NPR, 2006.

Horton, Alex, 2019, "Ohio Republican Blames Mass Shootings on 'Drag Queen Advocates,' Colin Kaepernick and Obama," *The Washington Post*. Accessed August 10, 2019. https://www.washingtonpost.com/politics/2019/08/05/ohio-republican-blames-mass-shootings-drag-queen-advocates-colin-kaepernick-obama/?noredirect=on.

Murphy, Paul P., Konstantin Toropin, Drew Griffin, Scott Bronstein, and Eric Levenson, 2019, "Dayton Shooter Had an Obsession with Violence and Mass Shootings, Police Say," *CNN*. Accessed August 10, 2019. https://www.cnn.com/2019/08/05/us/connor-betts-dayton-shooting-profile/index.html.

Rucker, Philip, 2019, "'How Do You Stop These People?': Trump's Anti-Immigrant Rhetoric Looms over El Paso Massacre," *The Washington Post*. Accessed August 10, 2019. https://www.washingtonpost.com/politics/how-do-you-stop-these-people-trumps-anti-immigrant-rhetoric-looms-over-el-paso-massacre/2019/08/04/62d0435a-b6ce-11e9-a091-6a96e67d9cce_story.html.

Williams, Kevin, Hannah Knowles, Hannah Natanson, and Peter Whoriskey, 2019, "Gunman Killed Sister, Eight Others in Second Deadly U.S. Mass Shooting in 24 Hours," *The*

Washington Post. Accessed August 10, 2019. https://www.washingtonpost.com/nation/2019/08/04/nine-fatally-shot-dayton-including-suspect-day-after-mass-shooting-texas/.

Wong, Curtis M., 2018, "Pastor Blames California Wildfires on State's Embrace of Lgbtq Rights," *Huffington Post*. https://www.huffingtonpost.com/entry/kevin-swanson-california-wildfires_us_5b68552ae4b0de86f4a391ae.

CROSSCURRENTS

THE FIRST #METOO ACTIVISTS
Contemporary Campaigning in Support of the Former Japanese Military "Comfort Women"

Caroline Norma

Activists today continue to rally around the history of the Japanese military's sexual enslavement of women and girls in the China and Pacific wars of the 1930s and 1940s. Their activism is undertaken mostly to extract state-level apology and reparation from the Japanese government for these crimes of enforced prostitution or "military sexual slavery." It is undertaken on behalf of, together with, and in the name of survivors and their descendants. Recently, though, with declining numbers of elderly former "comfort women" able to join campaigning, there have emerged other rationales for continuing with the movement for justice. South Korean activists now mobilize against "sexual violence in war" wherever it occurs in the world, as reflected in an installation of the War and Women's Human Rights Museum in Hongdae that commemorates, in spite of its name, specifically the history of Japanese military sexual slavery and activism by survivors. Walking through the museum, visitors eventually end up on a floor exhibiting crimes of sexual violence in conflicts like that in the Congo. This framing of the contemporary movement aligns with international efforts to spotlight crimes of rape in war, which recently culminated in the awarding of the 2018 Nobel Peace Prize to a doctor and a survivor who have "helped to give greater visibility to war-time sexual violence."

We might well worry about wartime sexual violence in countries like the Congo, but, in this article, I question this framework for "comfort women" campaigning. It dilutes and diverts political action that might otherwise produce good results in contemporary Northeast Asia for women and children, I argue; in suppressing the region's sex industries, for example. Further, the framework inadvertently replicates overly broad castings of the "comfort women" issue that are favored by defenders of the country's wartime record, like that of Japan's current Prime Minister Abe Shinzou. In a speech addressing the issue in 2007, he waxed lyrical that "[t]he 20th century was a century when human rights were violated in many parts of the world. So we have to make the 21st century a wonderful century in which no human rights are violated." Reframing the criminality of the Japanese military's prostitution system as a problem of "sexual violence in war" weakens, furthermore, the movement's effectiveness, because campaigners are not usually residing in countries plagued by war, let alone crimes of wartime rape, I suggest. In other words, as Samuel Moyn criticizes of contemporary "human rights" campaigners who rally around crimes of states abroad while overlooking serious problems of inequality in their own societies (2012), framing the problem as one of "rape in war" sloughs the history of Japanese military sexual slavery from the reality of contemporary Northeast Asia and estranges it from large-scale industries of female sexual exploitation operating in countries like Japan, which, I believe, are relevant and important targets of campaigning if we accurately understand the historical cause of what the "comfort women" endured (Moyn 2012).

The historical cause of what the "comfort women" endured is, in Rikkyo University historian Onozawa Akane's view, Japan's pre-war civilian sex industry (Onozawa 2010). In a 2010 monograph, she shows this industry operating cheek by jowl with the military's sexual slavery scheme. In line with this understanding of its origins, I argue that campaigning to suppress prostitution in contemporary times respects, and accurately reflects, the historical experience of survivors of military prostitution in its targeting of the historical cause of their enslavement, which is carried over today in the form of large-scale pornography and prostitution industries in Japan in particular (see Miyamoto 2016), as a threat to present-day women and girls, as they were in the girlhoods of survivors. Onozawa is not the only researcher to see the military prostitution system as historically attributable to Japan's pre-war civilian sex industry in this way, nor is my call for social movement mobilization in alignment with this understanding original. Later in the article, I describe the work of a number of other Japan-based historians and political theorists who arrive at the same conclusion.

The framing commended here already finds real-world expression in campaigns being undertaken by activists in Japan, which is a recent development not yet described in the literature. Their new approach to campaigning in solidarity with the former "comfort women" on the basis of opposition to Japan's contemporary sex industry is described here using Japanese-language publicity and advocacy materials produced by a range of activist groups in Tokyo and Osaka, one of which the author is a member (People Against Pornography and Sexual Violence, PAPS; see https://www.en.paps.jp/member). These groups have begun to direct their efforts in support of recognition and restitution for military sexual slavery survivors toward, as the Tokyo-based Violence Against Women in War Research Action Center (VAWW-RAC) declared in May 2017, "understanding schemes that continue to organise women for sexual violence in the present...[as] a means of addressing the problem of the Japanese military's 'comfort women' scheme of the past" (pamphlet on file with author) (VAWW-RAC 2017). In this approach, the sexual abuse and exploitation of women and girls in contemporary society is seen as manifesting the (prostitution-tolerant) social conditions that gave rise to the wartime military system in the first place. Further, it is seen as underwriting continuing Japanese government recalcitrance toward claims by military sexual slavery survivors (see Muta 2016). It is an advocacy strategy vastly different from that waged by campaigners in South Korea, both now and in the past. I describe this latter, mainstream approach before returning to the alternative approach of Japanese campaigners today. My argument is that while there is good reason to persist with campaigning over the history of wartime Japanese military sexual slavery beyond the lifetimes of its victims, to continue to have meaningful effect this justice movement must follow the lead of Japanese activists and become an abolitionist struggle against prostitution.

The "violence against women during armed conflict" paradigm
South Korean campaigning in support of the former "comfort women" has, at least since the 1990s, mostly eschewed consideration of military sexual slavery as a form of prostitution. This stance emerged partly in response to rhetoric by groups and individuals hostile to survivors. From

the mid-1990s, these were mostly based in Japan, and included even parliamentarians, but some were based in South Korea (see Kinoshita 2017). They defamed the "comfort women" as prostitutes who earned money as military camp-followers during the war, and not as victims of sexual violence. Their hostile characterizations led advocates early on to develop a counter-narrative emphasizing the non-prostituted status of survivors (see Norma 2017). As a result, an "e-museum" run by South Korea's Ministry of Gender Equality and Family today broadcasts the popularly progressive view that "comfort women were not the same as licensed prostitutes, but were victims of a state-run system of sexual violence," as shown in the purported fact that "the women had no free choice of where to live or freedom of movement," "[n]or did they have the liberty of quitting," which are key points of "differentiation from licensed prostitutes (Ministry of Gender Equality and Family, Republic of Korea)." This framing of survivors as anything but victims of prostitution is widely echoed by advocates, including by some in English-speaking countries. Out of consideration of survivors' alleged unwillingness to be tarred with the brush of prostitution, the judgment of the Women's International War Crimes Tribunal on Japan's Military Sexual Slavery mock trial held in Tokyo in 2000 to assess Japanese military and government responsibility for wartime crimes of military sexual slavery, for example, declared that

> [t]he identification of sexual slavery as an international crime in our Charter and as a matter of international law today is, in our opinion, a long overdue renaming of the crime of (en)forced prostitution. As such, it responds to a very important concern expressed by the survivors of the 'comfort system,' which is that the term 'forced prostitution' obscures the terrible gravity of the crime, suggests a level of voluntariness, and stigmatises its victims as immoral or 'used goods'...the effect to obscure the offence of sexual slavery by calling it prostitution did not end with the end of the war. Japan's sympathizers who deny its responsibility for the systematic atrocities perpetrated against the 'comfort women' and girls continue to characterise them as 'prostitutes' and 'camp followers' to assert both the voluntariness and immorality of the 'comfort women,' and thus Japan's own innocence.
>
> (2002, p. 150)

Out of concern that survivors might be hurt by being perceived as "prostitutes," in other words, the Tribunal judges in their final report coined the phrase "military sexual slavery" in order to "rename" less offensively the international legal understanding of the war crime of "enforced prostitution" that was established by the United Nations Commission in 1943 (see Friedmann and Jørgensen 2014, Plesch *et al.* 2014).

In the fifteen years since publication of this judgment, moreover, "sexual slavery" has come to exert weakening conceptual influence over the campaigning of South Korean advocates: Mohita Roman observed in 2011 that they now align themselves with a "global movement for the elimination of violence against women during armed conflict paradigm (Roman 2011)." Indeed, the website of the Tokyo-based advocacy group Kibou no Tane Kikin reports that South Korean survivors have set up charity funds for the Congo and Vietnam to support women who've had "the same experiences as them." (In the case of Vietnamese victims, this is likely to refer to women prostituted by South Korean troops during the Vietnam War.) Advocates in English-speaking countries follow their lead: Central Washington University's Bang-Soon Yoon at a 2015 counter-event held to protest his university's hosting of sexual slavery deniers from Japan lectured on "solidarity work done by the comfort women activists and their close allies in support of victims of military rape in other contexts around the globe, from the Eastern Congo to (most recently) Vietnam" (Auslander and Chong 2015). There is no doubting the good intentions behind these initiatives, but they produce a situation where the sex industry origins of the Japanese military's wartime brothel scheme are obscured through rejection of the United Nations 1943 "enforced prostitution" designation. Further, the scheme's own organization of women for prostitution is muddied in generalized characterizations of it as having arranged, broadly and indeterminably, "military rape" and sexual violence against women in war.

Japanese activists, too, it must be acknowledged, sometimes overlook the prostitution of the "comfort women" scheme in their contemporary campaigns. A photograph and primary materials exhibition held in Nago, Okinawa, in mid-October 2018 paired historical exhibits about comfort stations operating throughout the island chain during the war with information about the post-war sex crimes of U.S. military personnel stationed in Okinawa. While the exhibition impressively featured testimony from

300 victims of such U.S. military sexual violence, its failure to pair evidence of wartime military sexual slavery in Okinawa with examples of U.S. troops prostituting local women after the war is regrettable. There exists plentiful historical account of this prostitution (e.g., Höhn and Moon 2010, Sturdevant and Stoltzfus 1993). Instead, the exhibition adopted a "sexual violence in wartime" perspective, and Tsuji Akira, the curator of the community arts center that sponsored it, told reporters that the awarding of the Nobel Peace Prize to a doctor who had treated victims of sexual violence in conflict meant that "international attention...[was] beginning to focus on the issue of sexual violence in war," and so this had presented "an opportunity to re-visit what happened in Okinawa during the war" (Ianjo no jittai shoukai Okinawa senji seibouryoku tokubetsuten Okinawa Airakuen asu kara 2018). Revisiting the sexual enslavement of women in Okinawa during the war is of course a worthwhile endeavor, but the exhibition's design divorced this history from serious problems of U.S. military prostitution in post-war Okinawan society through associating the wartime "comfort women" scheme not with commercial sexual exploitation but with military sexual violence. Lost, therefore, was a chance to frame wartime and peacetime practices of military prostitution as comparable and equally condemnable forms of female sexual slavery.

Scholarly support for the South Korean approach
The generalized "sexual violence in armed conflict paradigm" finds support in the English-language literature, which is overwhelmingly concerned with "rape in war" and "rape as a weapon of war" rather than military prostitution or wartime sexual slavery. Outside the scholarship addressing the history of the "comfort women" scheme specifically, there exist few English-language works addressing military prostitution as sexual slavery. I was able to locate only four edited volumes evincing the approach, and even their chapters do not focus exclusively on military prostitution; they additionally canvass topics like wartime rape and problems of violence facing female military personnel (Barstow 2000, Drinck and Gross 2007, Hedgepeth and Saidel 2010, Stiglmayer et al. 1994). There are a number of volumes in English describing schemes of prostitution operating in settings of military occupation and around military bases (the best of which is Moon 1997), but these do not usually paint the

schemes as enacting female sexual slavery. Moreover, they emphasize the wrongness of *forced* military prostitution, rather than of military prostitution outright. Additionally, of course, there are numerous books describing prostitution in war and occupation that advance no understanding of it as a human rights abuse, let alone a practice enacting female sexual slavery (e.g., Anderson Hughes 2011, Dunbar 2014, Gaines 2014).

Outside the literature on the Japanese "comfort women" scheme, the volume in English that most forthrightly takes a stance against the prostitution of women in war as organizing female sexual slavery is an English-language edited collection translated from German titled *Forced prostitution in times of war and peace* (Drinck and Gross 2007). But, as is evident from its title, the book's editors distinguish "forced" and "free" forms of prostitution and frame "forced prostitution" as a "means of warfare" in the same way that wartime rape is popularly theorized as a "weapon of war." These editors suggest in their introduction that

> the entire area of sexual exploitation is used as a means of warfare, as it is capable of destroying people's identities so effectively—the identities of the women themselves and those of their whole families—and even constitutes a traumatic event for an entire nation.
>
> (p. 13)

If prostitution constitutes a weapon of war that can be traumatic for entire nations, the editors do not explain what function it then serves in peacetime societies, where it is usually more prevalent. But they do devote the book's first two chapters to discussing peacetime sex trafficking in Europe, even if this trafficking is distinguished from "willful" prostitution, as one of the chapter's authors is at pains to point out: "When I speak of forced prostitution, I am explicitly not speaking about prostitution!" (Boker 2007, p. 54). The English-language literature on military sexual slavery as a whole echoes her exclamatory determination to not speak about prostitution, and in this respect, it complements the campaigning approach of South Korean advocates.

Reluctance to see military prostitution as female sexual slavery, as I think marks the English-language literature, has recently come to influence the Japanese-language scholarship, which before now was differently dominated by a focus on female sexual slavery in respect of the historical "comfort women" scheme. This new influence likely arises out of the popularity of U.S. historian Mary Louise Roberts's monograph published in 2014, which was soon after translated into Japanese (Roberts 2014). (It is possible her book was translated so quickly into Japanese, and became so well known in Japan, because of its perceived usefulness to local right-wing groups in showing other militaries as having patronized brothels during the war, on the premise that a problem shared is a problem halved.) Roberts's book focuses on the sexual conduct of occupying American military personnel in France after the second war in Europe. She discusses their sexual violence alongside descriptions of non-violent, consensual relationships and marriages arising between them and local women. Her undifferentiated, generalized approach is praised in a 2018 Japanese-language volume edited by well-known feminist Ueno Chizuko, along with Araragi Shinzou and Hirai Kazuko, which replicates its methodology (Ueno et al. 2018). Their own introductory chapter suggests that rape, prostitution, love and marriage in war, and occupation should be understood in one theoretical basket to avoid casting women's role as that of victim. The three editors explain that

> the challenge of women's history is to 'restore women's agency to history' for those women who have been rendered powerless and objects of sacrifice in mainstream historical work. This is both an attempt to throw off a tendency within women's historical work to maintain a victim perspective in writing the history of women, as well as, on the other hand, to, even in a revisionist way, reveal the reality of women as perpetrators and accomplices.
>
> (p. xiii)

To avoid promoting any such "victim" perspective, the editors tacitly place prostitution on a continuum featuring wartime rape at one end, representing absent female "agency," and activities of heterosexual coupling at the other, representing the exercise of full agency, or at least that exercised in constrained circumstances. Along this continuum, military prostitution escapes designation as sexual slavery because it places somewhere between rape and marriage. In other words, female voluntarism, willingness, choice, and "agency" attach to it to a greater or lesser extent, and so its characterization as sexual slavery is put beyond consideration. Roberts in her 2014 book similarly conveys no view of military prostitution as sexual slavery; on the contrary, she describes occupying U.S.

military personnel prostituting local French women in neutral, if not whimsical, terms. Her recent influence on Japanese-language scholarship has, I think, caused this scholarship to depart from its former focus on the military prostitution of "comfort women" as an historical form of female sexual slavery. In contrast to this shift, though, as mentioned, there is movement underway in the opposite direction among Japan-based activist groups. These groups are changing their campaigning over the history of the "comfort women" to newly incorporate critiques of *contemporary* female sexual abuse and exploitation. This new development in Japan is described in the remainder of this article.

Contemporary campaigning in Japan over the history of military sexual slavery
It will seem perverse to be raising objection to activist and academic efforts against gendered atrocities like wartime rape and sexual violence against women in conflict. There is, after all, plentiful past and present evidence of military men perpetrating mass rapes and other non-prostitution sexual atrocities in conflict zones, including Japanese military men having inflicted widespread sexual violence on women in places like China during the war of the 1930s and 1940s. Distinguishing military prostitution and "sexual violence against women in war" is, moreover, an obviously fraught task: The recent abduction and long-term detention of Iraqi Yazidi and Nigerian Chibok women and girls in conflict zones for the purpose of mass gang rape, for example, might be difficult to describe as having taken the form of military prostitution. The two examples are, at the same time, inaccurately described as "wartime rape," given their obvious features of sexual slavery. Rectifying this definitional contradiction in helpfully lateral terms, Catharine MacKinnon offers the clarifying analysis that military sexual slavery "is at once both mass rape and serial rape in a way that is indistinguishable from prostitution," and that "prostitution is that part of everyday non-war life that is closest to what we see done to women in…war" (MacKinnon 1994, p. 191). She encourages us, in other words, to view civilian prostitution through a lens of military sexual slavery while concurrently identifying the prostitution elements of wartime sexual slavery schemes.

This abolitionist approach to understanding prostitution as a systematized form of male sexual violence against women and girls irrespective of its perpetration in times of war or peace rarely surfaces, though, in an academic and activist environment that prefers the generalized and de-sexualized "violence against women in armed conflict paradigm." The de-sexualization of even feminist analyses of military violence was noted by a team of researchers in 2018 that raised concerns about academics, aid workers, and policymakers ignoring the specifically sexual nature of the violence that is perpetrated against women in conflict zones:

> Wartime rape, as it is being framed in both the policy and academic world, is *decidedly not* about sex, sexual desire, pleasure, or sexuality. Very simply put, 'the sexual' (sexuality, desire, eroticism, etc.) has been seemingly *theorized away* as irrelevant, and even dangerously misleading in efforts to explain and redress conflict-related sexual violence. This erasure of the sexual accompanies the firm move to refute socio-biological explanations for wartime rape that located the 'cause' of sexual violence in male heterosexuality (their emphasis).
>
> (Baaz and Stern 2018, p. 295)

The all-too-familiar nature of the sexual violence perpetrated by men in war prompts inconvenient conclusions to be drawn about male heterosexuality in peacetime, the researchers suggest, and which academics, aid workers, and policymakers may be politically disinclined to pursue. This disinclination is likely motivated by many things, but reluctance to confront male heterosexuality in its familiar, local, peaceable guise possibly directs attention instead to forms of violence against women that are easily and specifically identifiable as products of war. The strategy is possibly less provocative; Tomoko Yamaguchi explains that, "[b]ased on my field research with Japanese neo-nationalists, the sexual nature of the 'comfort woman' issue seems to be a key factor in their resistance against official recognition that these crimes took place (Yamaguchi 2017)." We could speculate this is because recognizing the sexuality of wartime prostitution leads to questions about men's sexual conduct in peacetime, and so apologizing for historical forms of prostitution amounts to acknowledgment of the need for men to change their sexual behavior in present-day society.

Grassroots activists in Japan have nonetheless, as mentioned, adopted just such a view in their recent campaigning over the history of the "comfort women." They have come to newly focus on contemporary forms of male sexual exploitation and abuse of women and girls in efforts to pursue historical recognition and reparation for wartime victims. Their newly unique approach, broadly taking two forms, is described next.

Historical sexual slavery as an issue of sexual violence against women in contemporary Japan

Efforts by Japan-based activists to stress the relevance of contemporary forms of abuse and exploitation to the history of the wartime "comfort women" scheme have emerged only recently. The co-president of the Japan Women's and Human Rights Network, Kaori Sato, in 2018, for example, declared sexual violence, "including the past abuses against comfort women," a present-day issue for Japanese society, and emphasized the fact that "[o]ne out of every 15 Japanese females has suffered sexual violence, and 80% of the victims are children, adolescents, and young women" (in Cho 2018). But this tethering of "comfort women" campaigning to problems of contemporary sexual violence occurs, ironically, while the #MeToo movement in Japan is widely described as a failure (for this opinion, see, e.g., The Constitutional Democratic Party of Japan, 2018). This movement, which began in the United States in 2017 against men's workplace sexual harassment and assault of women, did not take off in Japan as it did in South Korea where large-scale rallies were held and court cases launched throughout 2018. Nonetheless, and perhaps ironically, the #MeToo framework continues to be deployed by Japanese activists in service of campaigns on behalf of the former "comfort women." Yang Jinja, who has for decades worked across a number of "comfort women" justice groups in the country, including as current director of Kibou no Tane Kikin (see https://www.kibotane.org/), said at a 2018 workshop that,

> [w]hen I first met Korea's 'comfort women' survivors, they were fighting an isolate, lonely battle. But the collective action of people who surrounded them turned these survivors into activists. These people supported the survivors in their #MeToo battle in a similar spirit to the #WithYou movement. It is this #WithYou movement that is lacking in Japan today.
>
> (workshop report on file with author)

In her comments, Yang characterizes the former "comfort women" as the world's "first #MeToo campaigners" for their public disclosures as survivors of male sexual violence, and their activist roles in rallying other women to the cause from the early 1990s. At the same workshop, though, longtime feminist campaigner and historian Kawada Fumiko spoke about her work from 1992 with a Japanese survivor (named Tami) and noted the inability of this survivor, in contrast, to come out publicly because no #WithYou movement existed to support her. Different from the survivors of Korean background that Yang describes as having the sympathy and support of activists in Japan and South Korea, and particularly that of Japan-resident Korean (*zainichi*) female activists, survivors of Japanese background like Tami did not attract solidarity and support because of their assumed historical association with prostitution (see Nishino *et al.* 2018).

Even with such problems afflicting the history of campaigning on behalf of sexual slavery survivors, and even while support for present-day sexual assault survivors is lacking in Japan, activists today nonetheless rally in support of the former "comfort women" under the #MeToo banner. An August 2018 workshop in Tokyo titled "The #MeToo movement that began with Kim Hak-sun," held to coincide with the August 14 comfort women international memorial day, featured speakers not only from groups active in the movement for the "comfort women" (and the event was jointly organized by two such groups), but also Tsunoda Yukiko who is a feminist lawyer involved for decades in advocacy and legal action on behalf of rape, pornography, and sexual harassment victims in the country. Tsunoda was formerly involved with the Anti-Prostitution and Pornography Research Group (APP), but more recently has begun consulting to Kibou no Tane Kikin, which, as above, is an NGO advocating justice for "comfort women." This example shows the combining of "comfort women" advocacy and campaigning over contemporary issues of sexual assault is undertaken not merely on rhetorical grounds: Japanese activists increasingly approach male sexual violence in the past and the present, and in wartime and peacetime, as a problem of the same nature.

This collaboration between groups representing different survivor cohorts (e.g., "comfort women," rape victims, or pornography industry survivors) now produces a range of jointly organized events, workshops, and publications. A November 2017 rally in Shibuya to mark the United Nations International Day to End Violence Against Women was organized by the National Movement for Resolving the Issue of the Japanese Military Comfort Women, which is a coalition encompassing around fifty civic groups including the Women's Active Museum on War and Peace (WAM).

WAM is another hub for activism and research in support of the former "comfort women" in Tokyo (see Szczepanska 2014). At the rally, participants announced that the "comfort women" issue was "a matter of women's rights, not diplomacy," and spoke out against a climate in Japan where women felt unable to disclose sexual victimization. They cited the example of women who were being forced to appear in pornographic videos in the country who blamed themselves for their own victimization on the basis they were at fault for having been deceived. This unfriendly climate for sexual violence victims in Japan was decried by rally participants as linked, furthermore, to Japanese government efforts to silence the comfort women (in Cho 2017). The Shibuya rally featured a diverse range of people and groups acting in coalition in support of the former "comfort women" and was a clear, early indication of a shift underway among activists Japan toward campaigning in support of wartime survivors on the basis of comprehension of links between different forms of male violence, including, crucially, prostitution and pornography in contemporary Japan.

This collaboration allows, furthermore, for participant groups to reflect on their commonalities, both positive and negative. The August 2018 workshop, for example, recognized Japanese women specifically as inadequately attracting public support, both as #MeToo survivors in the present and as "comfort women" in the past. The flyer for the workshop lamented Japan's women's movement as having failed the two cohorts. It featured a close-up head shot of the late Korean wartime survivor Kim Hak-sun alongside text that read:

> Unfortunately we cannot describe the so-called #MeToo movement as having taken off in Japan. Similarly, the movement that preceded the #MeToo wave involving women in a number of countries stepping forward as victims of the Japanese military's wartime 'comfort women' scheme failed to prompt women of Japanese nationality to step forward. These parallel events makes us wonder, 'Why are victims of sexual violence in Japan pressed this much into silence?' Why does the Japanese state never take steps to resolve its history of military sexual slavery? What should we do to cultivate a society that is intolerant of sexual violence?
> (Senjisei bouryoku mondai renraku kyougikai and Nihongun 'ianfu' mondai kaiketsu zenkoku koudou, 2018)

This sentiment is widely shared. Prior to the August workshop, in February 2018, Iikura Erii from the Tokyo University of Foreign Studies, at a joint ROK-Japan academic workshop on military prostitution held in Seoul, commented that insincere approaches taken by the Japanese government to the comfort women occur in conjunction with the re-victimization of #MeToo survivors in the country. Different from South Korean society, she continued, Japan's history of wartime sexual slavery, and the country's failure to reckon with it, had caused the #MeToo movement to falter. Iikura saw the different degrees of popularization of the #MeToo movement in Japan and South Korea as reflecting a gap between the two countries in terms of public consciousness about issues of gender and sexuality (Iikura 2018, p. 48). Iikura is likely correct in this observation; even surface-level indicators of women's status in the two countries, like the operation of a ministerial gender equality portfolio in South Korea that has never existed in Japan, seem to bear it out. There is no doubt Japanese feminists face a dispiriting situation in the country, in terms of both women's status and the campaigning environment needed to improve it. We might nonetheless see their efforts to pursue justice for victims of military sexual slavery, on a double bill with #MeToo activism, as a promising development, and one more politically viable than the approach currently pursued in South Korea where Roman's "violence against women during armed conflict paradigm" continues to hold sway. This paradigm, I suggest, leaves "comfort women" campaigning in that country bereft of contemporary relevance, particularly for young women as the movement's future leaders.

Even further than putting the "comfort women" on a double bill with #MeToo activism, moreover, Japanese feminist groups have recently begun combining their activities over military sexual slavery with critique of the country's sex industry. Loyal to Onozawa Akane's above-mentioned analysis, activists sound warning bells about prostitution and pornography in contemporary Japan as responsible for creating conditions similar to those that gave rise to the military "comfort women" system before the war. This approach to campaigning has emerged only in the last couple of years and will be shortly described, but its theoretical groundwork was laid long ago. Twenty years ago, Kokugakuin University's Morita Seiya published a journal article defining the military sexual slavery scheme as a problem of peacetime prostitution (Morita November 1999). Among other arguments in this vein, he wrote in 1999 that,

> [a]s long as the comfort women system is divorced from peacetime as a peculiar problem of war, or is understood exclusively as a product of the wayward activities of the Japanese military before the war, a true understanding of the system cannot be reached, and solutions found. The system is fundamentally linked to violence against, and the abuse of, women in Japan both before and after the war
>
> (p. 118)

Two years later, in a book chapter published in 2001, sociologist Suzuki 2001 made even more explicit reference to Japan's "contemporary rape/prostitution-tolerant culture" in discussing the wartime scheme and noted the scheme's links to civilian prostitution both before and after the war:

> The idea that girls sold into the [pre-war civilian sex] industry by their parents were exercising choice is incomprehensible ... it was a system of sexual slavery. If we are to identify the differences between the civilian legalised prostitution system and the comfort station system, we have to first acknowledge the slavery of the civilian system ... attempts to insist on differences between the two systems are likely to come from proponents who are capitalising on tenets of Japan's contemporary rape/prostitution-tolerant culture. It would be better to re-examine the comfort station system from the critical perspective of the rape/prostitution culture circulating in Japan in the pre-war period, as well as Japan's pre-war sex industry
>
> (p. 108)

A decade elapsed, though, before this understanding filtered down into the writings of activists and academics involved in campaigns to support the former "comfort women" in Japan, even if historians like Yamashita Yeong-ae did include early on in their work a sympathetic focus on prostituted women as victims of the military scheme (see, e.g., Yamashita & Yun, 1992). Among later academic activists, Nishino Rumiko was a strong advocate of the same view, and in 2010 recommended "[c]learly recognising and acknowledging the victimisation of [prostituted] Japanese 'comfort women'" as a means of "overcoming the gender prejudice that afflicts the 'comfort women' issue (Nishino 2010)." She suggested, in other words, that activists champion Japanese survivors specifically in their advocacy efforts on behalf of the former "comfort women" in order to break away from old, sexist ideas of prostitution as extinguishing claims to victimhood. Overcoming this prejudice and discriminatory way of thinking, which had afflicted the advocacy movement since its inception, and which had disenabled survivors of Japanese nationality stepping forward, would represent, Nishino believed, progress for both the movement and its survivors (p. 113).

This same commitment to prostituted and Japanese victims of the military scheme is upheld throughout the later work of historian Kinoshita Naoko, including in a 2018 book chapter where she critiques the framing that emerged early on, in the early 1990s, of military sexual slavery as a form of "forced trafficking." Kinoshita 2018 critiques this framing, firstly, as having resulted in a denial of justice for victims who were perceived as failing to meet the standard set by the concept because of personal histories of prostitution and, secondly, as having obscured the reality of the "comfort women" scheme as a system of sexual violence that grew out of Japan's licensed brothel sector. Kinoshita calls for wholesale re-evaluation of the testimony of survivors, and reconsideration of the harms that historical prostitution systems have done to women, not only in Japan but also in Korea and other countries where military sexual slavery victims were originally targeted and recruited (p. 82). Kinoshita's 2018 discussion goes further than other academic accounts of the issue in its theorizing of a direction for advocacy campaigning and politics, and, since advancing this analysis, her approach has begun to find real-world manifestation in the activism of feminist and other civic groups in Japan. Examples of it are described next.

Wartime sexual slavery as an issue of the sexual exploitation of women in contemporary Japanese society
The groups Women's Active Museum on War and Peace (WAM) and Violence Against Women in War Research Action Center (VAWW-RAC) lead research and activist efforts in Japan in support of the former "comfort women." The groups maintain leading-edge approaches to the issue in both their theorizing and campaigning, and since 2015, their members have focused on Japanese women specifically as victims of the wartime scheme irrespective of their prior prostituted status. Questioning the exclusion of these women from the broader movement in support of

survivors, VAWW-RAC members have published a number of volumes arguing in favor of their recognition and advancement (see, most recently, Nishino *et al.* 2018), and in July 2018, VAWW-RAC members, including Yoshimi Yoshiaki, Kim Puja, Onozawa Akane, and journalist Okamoto Yuuki, traveled to South Korea to meet with like-minded colleagues. Significantly, the like-mindedness of these activist colleagues arose not from their similar advocacy on behalf of the former "comfort women," such as the Korean Council for the Women Drafted for Military Sexual Slavery by Japan (who of course VAWW-RAC already had historically strong links with), but from their involvement in efforts against prostitution and the sex industry. In other words, activists who have worked over the past two decades to bring about South Korea's anti-prostitution laws of 2004, and subsequently to run government-subsidized shelter and welfare facilities to aid women's exit from the local sex industry, were the colleagues VAWW-RAC members traveled to meet. Among other people, the delegates visited the director of Salim Center, Byun Jeonghee, in Pusan, which has been a hub of feminist anti-prostitution organizing and thinking in South Korea (together with the group National Solidarity for Resolving the Problem of Prostitution) since its founding by feminist activists at the turn of the century.

Crucial to the cultivation of these connections with South Korea's feminist anti-prostitution movement has been the activism and journalism of Kitahara Minori who is involved in a range of groups in Tokyo, including Kibou no Tane Kikin and PAPS. As a journalist, Kitahara has traveled to South Korea numerous times to interview anti-prostitution activists and to document developments in South Korean legal and activist efforts against the local sex industry. Kitahara's work has facilitated VAWW-RAC's connection to these activists, who are a group apart from advocates attached to groups in coalition with the Korean Council. The July 2018 trip was significant and unique for its different focus on South Korea's anti-prostitution policy and infrastructure, rather than activism and organizations in direct and exclusive support of the former "comfort women." VAWW-RAC members were not originally involved in abolitionist efforts in Japan (Anti-Pornography and Prostitution Research Group members were earliest involved in these efforts), but increasingly the organization sponsors PAPS members like Miyamoto Setsuko to speak at their seminars, as happened in May 2017. At that

VAWW-RAC seminar, Miyamoto spoke about her newly released book on Japan's contemporary sex industry.

Soon afterward, in July 2017, VAWW-RAC member and historian Onozawa Akane was written up in dialogue with Kitahara Minori in the magazine *Shuukan Kinyoubi* (Onozawa and Kitahara 2017). This piece was specifically about the exploitation of young women in pornography production in Japan. It came about because of Kitahara's membership of PAPS, connection with *Shuukan Kinyoubi*, and her ground-level knowledge of problems relating to the sexual exploitation of young women in Japan. It was significant that Onozawa, as one of Japan's leading historians of the "comfort women" system, chose to join Kitahara in commenting on the issue as an area relevant to her expertise. Indeed, in the piece, Onozawa makes the historically informed point that techniques of trickery used by pornographers in contemporary Japan to trap young women for the purpose of pornography filming are similar to the strategies that were used by pimps in Japan's past, in places like the country's pre-war licensed prostitution districts (which is Onozawa's area of historical expertise). In *Shuukan Kinyoubi*, Onozawa further critiqued tolerance toward prostitution evident over the course of Japanese history and argued this tolerance promoted the development of the wartime comfort women system (p. 29). Then, referring to current-day forced pornography filming specifically, Onozawa criticized the fact that Japanese society does not currently problematize pornography unless there is evidence of clear force involved in its production. She noted the same problem afflicts the history of the "comfort women." Particularly for Japanese survivors who were often in prostitution before entering the military system, there is a tendency to deny their victimhood, she argued, in spite of all prostitution in Japan during the war years being organized through trafficking, and as having been organized wholly on the basis of force (i.e., in the form of underage girls entering prostitution venues). Even the slightest hint of any self-direction in the histories of victims straight away renders them no longer victims, she added, and this problem is common to both the former comfort women and contemporary victims of Japan's sex industry. Onozawa suggested that this commonality is caused by "male belief in the right to buy women for prostitution," and therefore to see the sex industry as a mere venture of business. "I really think we need to think more broadly about the context in which young women today might enter the sex industry—what is behind their decisions, their contexts of poverty, and the society they live in which sees prostitution as natural and inevitable," Onozawa suggested in conclusion to her statements (p. 31).

It is significant that Onozawa, as one of Japan's most prolific historians of the wartime sexual slavery scheme, would highlight so clearly similarities between the situation of women she had researched in depth for their wartime prostitution experience, and young women in today's Japan who are recruited by a sex industry that is, on its surface, "free" and very different from the pimps, brokers, and traffickers of the sex industry of Japan's war days. But the fact that Onozawa was able to so readily observe such similarities reflects, I believe, the sophistication and broad-mindedness of the activist movement in Japan advocating on behalf of the former "comfort women."

Conclusion

Japanese feminists have attracted some criticism, including from this author (Norma 2017), for their historical failure since the 1990s to build a movement within Japan in support of Japanese and other prostituted survivors of the wartime military "comfort women" scheme (see also Kinoshita 2017). Instead of taking up the cause of local victims living in Japan, these activists from early on followed the lead of South Korean campaigners and focused on victims abroad, which meant the global movement in support of survivors was delayed by more than a decade as South Korean activists waited out the years of military dictatorship to restart justice campaigning after the revolution of 1987. It also meant that Japanese victims were deprioritized in campaigning in favor of Korean victims and other survivors living outside of Japan. Yoshitake Teruko, one of the founders in 1975 of the Tokyo-based Group of Activist Women, has written about how the presence of a military regime in Korea made it difficult for information about the "comfort women" to be transmitted to Japan while, simultaneously, feminist campaigning was preoccupied with opposing other issues of sexism within Japan, which retarded the growth of the "comfort women" justice movement there (in Koudou suru Onnatachi No Kai, 1999, p. 237). This was unfortunate for survivors of Japanese nationality who were almost never able to come forward, let alone be recognized as victims or awarded restitution.

Whatever our view of this history, though, the discussion of this article has differently and hopefully noted a radical and promising break from the past undertaken by Japanese feminists and their allied campaigners. The justice movement in Japan now moves in a very different direction toward squarely and actively facing the country's history of military sexual slavery from a critical perspective on sexual exploitation and abuse in present-day Japan. In Japan today, the country's women and children are seriously affected by sex industrialization, commercial sexualization, and industries promoting underage sexual exploitation. But, even while the #MeToo movement is seen as having failed in the country, feminist activists have begun campaigning in support of the former "comfort women" from a stance of critique of Japan's sex industry, and its exploitation of young women in contemporary Japan in the same way wartime survivors were tricked and manipulated. This renovates the movement in support of restitution and recognition for victims of wartime sexual slavery through making their plight one of contemporary relevance for current-day Japanese women and girls. Through this framing of the movement, Japanese activists are successfully renewing the struggle and ensuring its successful future in coming decades as new cohorts of young women take up the struggle against sexual slavery from a position of opposition to sexual slavery enacted before their eyes in peacetime society.

Works cited

Anderson Hughes, Jessica R. 2011 Forced Prostitution: The Competing and Contested Uses of the Concentration Camp Brothel. 2011.

Auslander, Mark, and Chong Eun Ahn, 2015 '"Responding to "Comfort Woman" Denial at Central Washington University', The Asia-Pacific Journal, Vol. 13, Issue 22, No. 3, June 1, 2015 at https://apjjf.org/Mark-Auslander/4325.html

Baaz ME, Stern M. 2018, "Curious erasures: the sexual in wartime sexual violence," International Feminist Journal of Politics **20**(3), pp. 295–314.

Barstow AL. 2000. War's Dirty Secret: Rape, Prostitution, and other Crimes against Women. Cleveland, OH: Pilgrim Press.

Boker, Marion 2007 Forced prostitution in Europe', pp. 53-66 in Drinck, Barbara and Gross, Chung-Noh. *Forced prostitution in times of war and peace: sexual violence against women and girls*, Bielefeld, Germany, 2007.

Cho, Giwon, 2018 'Nihon de ianfu higaisha memoriaru deii kinen gyouji kaisai,' *Hankyoreh*, 12 August 2018 at http://japan.hani.co.kr/arti/international/31332.html

Cho, Ki-weon, 2017 'Japanese civic groups hold candlelight rally over comfort women issue,' *Hankyoreh*, 27 November 2017 at http://english.hani.co.kr/arti/english_edition/e_international/820908.html

Drinck Barbara, Gross Chung-Noh. 2007. Forced Prostitution in Times of War and Peace: Sexual Violence Against Women and Girls. Germany: Bielefeld.

Dunbar Raden. 2014. The Secrets of the ANZACS: The Untold Story of Venereal Disease in the Australian Army, 1914–1919. Brunswick, Melbourne, Vic: Scribe Publications.

Friedmann, Danny, and Jørgensen Nina H.B. 2014 Enforced Prostitution in International Law Through the Prism of the Dutch Temporary Courts Martial at Batavia(December 12, 2014). M. Bergsmo, Cheah W.L. and Yi P. (eds.) Historical Origins of International Criminal Law, (TOAEP, Torkel Opsahl Academic EPublisher, 2014) at https://ssrn.com/abstract=2569174

Gaines J. 2014. An Evening with Venus: Prostitution during the American Civil War. Buffalo Gap, TX: State House Press.

Hedgepeth Sonja M., Saidel Rochelle G. 2010. Sexual Violence against Jewish Women during the Holocaust. Waltham, MA: Brandeis University Press.

Höhn Maria, Moon Seungsook. 2010. Over There: Living with The U.S. Military Empire From World War Two to the Present. Durham, NC: Duke University Press.

Ianjo no jittai shoukai Okinawa senji seibouryoku tokubetsuten Okinawa Airakuen asu kara 2018 Ryuukyuu Shimpou, 12 October 2018, https://ryukyushimpo.jp/news/entry-817489.html

Iikura, Erii, 2018 'Nikkan beigun kichi to sei baibai: rekishi to seisaku part 1,' pp. 42–49, *Kikan Sensou Sekinin Kenkyuu*, Vol. 90, Summer 2018.

Kinoshita Naoko. 2017. 'Ianfu' mondai no gensetsu kuukan: Nihonjin 'ianfu' no fukashika to genzen. Tokyo: Bensei Shuppan.

Kinoshita, Naoko, 2018pp. 65-83 in Ueno Chizuko, Araragi Shinzou and Hirai Kazuko, *Sensou to seibouryoku no hikakushi e mukete*, Iwanami Shoten, Tokyo, 2018.

Koudou Suru Onnatachi No Kai, ed. 1999. Koudou suru onnatachi ga hiraita michi. Tokyo: Miraisha.

MacKinnon, Catharine A. 1994 Feminism Unmodified: Discourses on Life and Law. Cambridge, MA: Harvard University.

Ministry of Gender Equality and Family, Republic of Korea, 'I'm the evidence': e-museum of the Japanese military sexual slavery, http://actionforpeace.net/sub.asp?pxml:id=226

Miyamoto Setsuko. 2016. AV shutsuen o kyouyousareta kanojotachi. Tokyo: Chikuma Shobou.

Moon, Katharine. 1997. Sex Among Allies: Military Prostitution in U.S.-Korea Relations. New York: Columbia University Press.

Morita Seiya. November 1999, "Senji no sei bouryoku heiji no sei bouryoku," Yuibutsuron Kenkyuu Nenshi **4**, pp. 113–140.

Moyn Samuel. 2012. The Last Utopia: Human Rights in History. Cambridge, MA: Belknap Press of Harvard University Press.

Muta Kazue. 2016, "The 'Comfort Women' Issue and the Embedded Culture of Sexual Violence in Contemporary Japan," Current Sociology **64**(4), pp. 620–636.

Nishino, Rumiko, 2010 'Josei kokusai senpan houtei wa Nihonjin "ianfu" o dou ichi duketaka,' pp. 103-122 in Oogoshi, Aiko and Igeta, Midori, *Gendai feminizumu no eshikkusu*, Seikyuusha Tokyo, 2010.

Nishino Rumiko, Kim Puja, and Onozawa Akane. 2018. Denying The Comfort Women: The Japanese State's Assault on Historical Truth. New York London: Routledge/Taylor & Francis Group.

Norma, Caroline. 2017. "Abolitionism in the History of the Transnational "Justice for Comfort Women Movement" In Japan And South Korea" in Patrick Finney ed., Remembering the Second World War, Routledge, pp. 115–139.

Onozawa Akane. 2010. Kindai nihon shakai to koushou seido: Minshuushi to kokusai kankeishi no shiten kara. Tokyo: Yoshikawakoubunkan.

Onozawa, Akane, and Kitahara Minori, 2017, "Thinking About Coercion in the Context of Prostitution: Japan's Military 'Comfort Women' and Contemporary Sexually-Exploited Women," The Asia-Pacific Journal Japan Focus **15**(19), p. 4.

Plesch Dan, SaCouto Susana, Lasco Chante. 2014, "The Relevance of the United Nations War Crimes Commission to the Prosecution of Sexual and Gender-Based Crimes Today," Criminal Law Forum **25**, pp. 12–14.

Roberts Mary Louise. 2014. What Soldiers Do: Sex and the American GI in World War II France. Chicago: University of Chicago Press.

Roman Mohita. 2011. Framing the Korean 'comfort Women' Movement: Domestic Constraints and Transnational Alignments, PhD thesis.

Senjisei bouryoku mondai renraku kyougikai and Nihongun 'ianfu' mondai kaiketsu zenkoku koudou 2018 groups-sponsored 14 August 2018, 'Kim Haksun-san kara hajimatta #MeToo,' seminar for Memorial Day for Japanese Forces' Comfort Women Victims, flyer on file with author.

Stiglmayer Alexandra, Faber Marion, Gutman Roy. 1994. Mass Rape: The War against Women in Bosnia-Herzegovina. Lincoln: University of Nebraska Press.

Sturdevant Saundra Pollock, Stoltzfus Brenda. 1993. Let the Good Times Roll: Prostitution and the U.S. Military in Asia. New York: New Press.

Suzuki, Masahirou, 2001 'Sensou ni okeru dansei no sekushuaritii,' pp. 108–117 in Ningen to Sei Kyouiku Kenkyuu kyougikai Dansei Keisei Kenkyuu Purojekuto, *Nihon no otoko wa doko kara kite doko e iku no ka: Dansei sekushuariti keisei kyoudou kenkyuu*, Tokyo: Juugatsusha, 2001.

Szczepanska Kamila. 2014. The Politics of War Memory in Japan: Progressive Civil Society Groups and Contestation of Memory of the Asia-Pacific War. Abingdon, Oxon; New York, NY: Routledge.

The Constitutional Democratic Party of Japan, 2018 'Nihon-ban parite de towareru no wa, watashitachi no ishi desu,' 20 December 2018 at https://cdp-japan.jp/interview/19

Ueno, Chizuko, Araragi Shinzo, and Hirai Kazuko, 2018 'Hajime ni,' pp. v-xviii in Ueno Chizuko, Araragi Shinzou and Hirai Kazuko, *Sensou to seibouryoku no hikakushi e mukete*, Iwanami Shoten, Tokyo, 2018.

Violence Against Women in War Research Action Center (VAWW-RAC), 2017 event promotion flyer, 13 May 2017, on file with author.

Women's International War Crimes Tribunal for the Trial of Japan's Military Sexual Slavery, 2002 'Judgement on the Common Indictment and the Application for Restitution and Reparation,' Violence Against Women in War Network Japan, Tokyo, 2002.

Yamaguchi, Tomoko, 2017 'The "Japan Is Great!" Boom, Historical Revisionism, and the Government,' *The Asia-Pacific Journal*, Vol. 15, Issue 6, No 3., 15 March 2017 at https://apjjf.org/2017/06/Yamaguchi.html

Yamashita Yeong-ae, Yun Chung-ok. 1992. Chousenjin josei ga mita ianfu mondai: Asu o tomo ni tsukuru tame ni. Tokyo: *San'ichi Shobou*.

CROSSCURRENTS

INTERVIEW WITH DR. ROBERT ORSI (NORTHWESTERN UNIVERSITY)

Samuel B. Davis and Pamela D. Winfield

1. What is the working title of your next book? How are you approaching this sensitive topic, and why is this an important contribution to the field?

The title of the book I'm working on right now is *Give Us Boys*, which is the first half of a phrase attributed by Voltaire to Saint Ignatius Loyola, founder of the Society of Jesus. The rest of the phrase is alleged to have been something like, "and we give them back to you as men." But it is likely that Voltaire himself coined the phrase as a comment on what he had come to see as the Jesuits' pedagogical pretensions (Voltaire himself was a product of Jesuit education). The Jesuits are famous, of course, for their educational institutions, at which some of the most powerful and influential men in modern history have been trained—three members of the current US Supreme Court, for instance, and 16% of the Congress. Look at the leadership both of South American fascism and of the resistance to it (including Fidel Castro) and you will find men trained by Jesuits. *Give Us Boys* examines the formation—the Catholic word for the deep and transformative care of mind, body, and soul—of a class of young men at a Jesuit prep school in the Bronx in 1967–1971. The boys came to the school from different ethnic and class backgrounds, from city neighborhoods and from the wealthy northern suburbs. It was an exciting time in Catholicism, just after the Second Vatican Council, following the terrible betrayal that *Humanae Vitae* was to the hopes generated by the meetings in Rome, and the first stirrings of reaction. It was also a convulsive time in the city and nation, when a racist discourse of fear was deployed to dismiss progressive initiatives in favor of police solutions in a neoliberal context. So, the book looks at formation as it is intersected by these diverse realities.

But what may make the book somewhat unusual is its insistence on the centrality of sexuality to this history, and more broadly to modern Catholicism, and therefore, more broadly, to the modern world. The history of modernity, and in particular the history of sexual modernity, cannot be told apart from Catholicism, although this may strike many as counterintuitive. *Give Us Boys* aims to be a new kind of Catholic history, one in which sexuality is not peripheral, nor set apart in a sphere of its own, but central, as I argue sexuality was to Catholicism throughout modernity. Historians of Catholicism seem to have succumbed to what I am thinking of these days as the celibacy fallacy, meaning that the men and women they are studying were actually living in faithfulness to their vows. Don't get me wrong: many were. But very many weren't, at different times and in various places. It's time that we put sexuality fully into the study of the history of Catholicism (as Foucault, who grew up Catholic, would agree). And I don't mean in the sense of prohibitions, but of the dynamic between prohibition and permission, of the interplay of denial and desire and what comes of it.

Catholicism was the sexual closet of the modern world. Think of global modernity along the lines of a metaphor of a house. You have different rooms, with different functions, arranged differently in various contexts...We know, for instance, that democracy looks different in say, Iran, then it does in Italy, or in Argentina. So, too, freedom of religion. Still, imagine this big and various house called "modernity" and then be aware that in it, at its center, is a great sexual closet. That is Catholicism. From Rimbaud to Mapplethorpe and beyond. Out of this closet came perversities and pleasures, prohibitions and permissions; out of the closet came beauty and horror. From Quebec to Ireland to the Catholic missions in Africa, across South America, the Catholic closet made sexuality horribly dangerous for women, for children, for the vulnerable, even as it put into place immense institutions to care for the victims it helped create. As the clergy sexual abuse crisis has taught us, Catholic authorities are willing to sacrifice anything for the preservation of their sexual regime.

I can't say how my work is a contribution to "the field," whatever the field is; such a judgment belongs to the field itself.

2. What is the relationship between your current work with Catholic sex abuse survivors and your prior work? What are the similarities? Differences?

My mother, who died sixteen years ago, has been much on my mind these days. She was a fiercely Catholic woman, who held together a deep and abiding love for Jesus, Mary and the saints, with the deepest scorn for the pretensions of clerical and prelatical authority. She is probably the clue to what links the various periods of my work together: I have always been concerned with Catholics lived experience—Italian immigrants despised by the Irish American church; women who turned to Saint Jude as a way of contending not only with the everyday realities of their respective times—war, economic distress, the dangers of childbirth, sickness—but also with the impositions of male clerical authority. Think of the cruelties of the Quebec church or the Irish, or the southern Italian, or the Chilean—it goes on and on and on. I have always been interested in people who struggle against this to make lives for themselves in the ontology into which they were born and formed. People sometimes say to me, well, couldn't these people upon whom the authority and cruelty of the male authorities of the church weighed so heavily simply leave? But why should they? What sort of question is this? To borrow a phrase from de Certeau, I'm interested in those who insist on a right to Catholicism, akin to his "right to the city," those who refuse the authority of those who would deny them access, and will not leave.

A Catholic priest recently asked me what he could do in response to my critique; if one accepts my analysis, he said, how is one to be a priest. First, let me say that while I reject any assumption that there are "innocent priests" unaware of the abuses of power taking place around them, I welcomed his openness. I said that he might consider saying mass on Sunday mornings outside the church building, on its steps, to show that there is a Catholicism bigger than that contained within the walls of the institution and its fantasies of power. If he does this, I will go back to mass.

3. What does your research actually entail? What are the challenges and opportunities of working with survivor support groups? How do you negotiate that space, and how have you been welcomed into it (or not)?

My research is a combination of ethnography and historical study; I work with documents and in archives, and I work in conversation with living persons. Survivors have welcomed me because they want their stories to be part of the historical record, and they know all too well that Catholic authorities are doing all in their power to erase them now. There has been nothing to negotiate. It has been a foundational axiom of my work over the years that I am responsible for representing as carefully, directly and straightforwardly as possible the people—in the past or in the present—among whom I go in order to understand some aspect of Catholicism, and by extension, of religion itself, in the modern world. I am always careful to use their language for their experience, and to pay attention to how they understand themselves, the ideas they have about themselves. But how I understand them in relation to the historical and phenomenological questions I ask is my responsibility to myself and to my colleagues in the academy. I take very, very seriously the importance of the latter as my primary interlocutors.

4. When did your research start, and have you noticed any shift in survivor attitudes given the media attention over the years? (For example, the summer of 2017 has often been called "the summer of shame." Have you seen a difference, or a shift, in the attitudes of the people you have talked to since then?)

Survivors I know are afraid Catholic authorities will succeed in erasing them, in convincing the public, both within the church and outside it, that they, these authorities, have adequately dealt with the problem (before they, the authorities, have even understood the problem or acknowledged it) by putting in place some simple programs for protecting children, as if any protocols will be effective against the ontological presumptions of men who are given the authority to bind and loosen. Even the fact that so many were "shocked" by the Pennsylvania report: it's like the scene in "Casablanca" where the police commissioner is "shocked" that gambling is going on at Rick's establishment. The survivors are good and sick of the willful naivete of Catholics who persist in thinking this crisis is being adequately dealt with or that it is in the past. "Naivete" is a compliment. For some, like the reactionaries in the Vatican, they are knowingly distorting the realities of what they insist on calling a "crisis" when it is really, as I have argued elsewhere, the everyday normal of modern Catholicism.

5. What does your question, "What is Catholic about the Catholic Sex Abuse Crisis," mean? If sexual abuse is something that exists within many communities, why is it important to specify the "Catholic" nature of this particular crisis?

Catholic authorities and their lawyers prefer to talk about the "crisis" as one of pedophilia, insisting that there is no difference between a priest and, say, Larry Nassar. This argument alone, which is truly beneath contempt, shows the full corruption of Catholic authorities in regards to this situation. As a survivor I spoke to whom I have identified elsewhere as Monica said, every person sexually abused by a priest was abused in a Catholic way. Abusers drew on the imagery and theology of Catholicism for staging their sexual actions, for explaining them to themselves and their victims, and the abuse took place within the rich aesthetic, sacramental, ontological environment of lived Catholicism. It cannot be separated from it. To say this is not to deny that there is much to be learned from other religious contexts about religious sexual violence, nor that insights from Catholic experience might not be useful elsewhere. But particularity matters.

6. How do you respond to questions about the causes of the crisis, and about its possible solutions or responses?

It's not a "crisis." It's the modern Catholic normal. It's causes need to be studied locally and globally, in their theological and doctrinal grounds, as well as in the pathologies of sexual violence. Catholic clerical misogyny is key to all of this. I don't see how any thinking person can read John Paul II's celebrations of "marriage" and "woman" without seeing he is both ignorant and terrified about both. And always, whatever he says about sexuality must be viewed in relation to his staunch defense of Marcial Maciel, a malignant sexual predator and rapist. "Woman"—those defenses of ethereal womanhood (while, by the way, he himself was in a complicated relationship with a real woman)—served as a screen for his defense of one of the most depraved figures in the history of the church. And for this the College of Cardinals saw fit to canonize John Paul II. This is what I mean when I say this was the Catholic normal. But the question is too broad: we need decades of particular research now, on the dynamics and contexts of particular instances of sexual violence by priests, in the US and elsewhere, before we can begin talking about causes. It is not my responsibility to offer "solutions" or "responses."

7. Where does work on Catholic sex abuse fit in the overall scheme of religious studies? How does it pose challenges to our writing, teaching, and thinking about religion?

I'm not sure what the "scheme of religious studies" means. As I have said, I hope that we will see, post-Catholic sexual abuse "crisis," that sexuality is not peripheral to the study of religion, but integral to it.

BOOK

BEST OF BROTHERS, FINEST OF MEN, OR ...?

Joseph and the Way of Forgiveness: A Biblical Tale Retold. Stephen Mitchell, New York, NY: St. Martin's Essentials, 2019 254pp. $21.99.

It's hard to think of a literary genre that the versatile, prodigiously learned, and widely acclaimed Stephen Mitchell has *not* ventured into: poetry and fiction, non-fiction, translations (of everything from *Gilgamesh* to Homer to Rilke) and adaptations (from eight languages), compilations of all sorts, including "sacred prose and poetry," and even children's books—about four dozen volumes in all, some of them in collaboration with his wife Byron Katie.

The bulk of his work has centered on the classics, both ancient and modern, and religion, from Hinduism to Buddhism to Judaism to Christianity. This time around he has chosen to do a contemporary Midrashic version of the story of Joseph, a tale that, Mitchell reminds us, Tolstoy thought the most beautiful in the world, with a hero whom he calls "the most spiritually mature character in the Hebrew Bible." Jack Miles said as much in *God: A Biography* (1996), but then the Old Testament seldom engages in hagiography (cf. the way Moses was banned, for an obscure minor lapse, from entering the Promised Land). In fact, the Hebrew Bible specialized in warts-and-all portraiture long before that phrase became popular in the 18th century. Mitchell makes a compelling case for the moral greatness of Joseph, with a little help from laudatory early rabbinical commentary. But the Bible, like the Talmud, always leaves room for contrary voices; and while joining Mitchell in his warm, affectionate, compelling account, we can still ask a few edgy questions.

Mitchell actually begins on a misleading note, when he writes that the previously, and agonizingly, barren Rachel welcomes her newborn son by naming "the boy Joseph, which means He Has Taken Away (that is, God Has Taken Away My Humiliation)." Well, she did thank God for taking away what the KJV calls her "reproach" (Gen. 30.24); but the actual etymology of the name means "let him [the god] add," (from the verb *yasaf*) as Rachel herself acknowledges when she immediately proclaims, "The LORD shall add [or 'May the LORD add'] to me another son" (Gen. 30.24). Then too, Mitchell occasionally refers to the "Jews," which is unhistorical, because the ancient Hebrews or Israelites weren't called Jews until long after the reduction of Israel to the southern kingdom of Judah in 721 BCE.

Oh well, no big deal. The authors of midrash can take all sorts of liberties. For example, the biblical story of Joseph fuses two different versions, in one of which it's Simeon who saves

Joseph's life from his murderous brethren; in the other it's Judah. Mitchell opts for Judah, which among other things lets him make good use of the seemingly ill-placed narrative of Judah and Tamar in Chapter 38. The original text likewise provides two alternative groups of traders, Ishmaelites and Midianites, who buy Joseph and take him to Egypt to sell him as a slave. Mitchell chooses the Ishmaelites, perhaps because of the link with the fateful events surrounding the lives of Isaac and Ishmael, the chosen and the exiled offspring of Abraham.

He breaks up his meditation on Joseph into more than a hundred very brief chapters, combining two things the Bible seldom has time for: detailed descriptions of the thoughts, emotions, and self-analyses of both major and minor characters. Practically everyone here, from Jacob and Joseph to his brothers to Potiphar's wife is torn by guilt or some painful inner conflict—all of which will be resolved in the end.

Mitchell obviously isn't going to aim for the gargantuan proportions of Thomas Mann's *Joseph and His Brothers*, which took sixteen years to write (roughly 1926-1942) and is over 1,500 pages long in John E. Woods's splendid translation. (Mitchell never even mentions Mann, which seems odd.) But he expands the original with many invented episodes and his own reflections. Among the former, Joseph's brothers savagely thrash him before flinging him into a ditch to wallow in his own urine and feces. Mitchell makes Potiphar a eunuch (so does Mann), which is reasonable enough, given that high officials in the ancient world (like the baptized Ethiopian who was the treasurer of Queen Candace in Acts 8.27) were frequently eunuchs, although the Egyptians apparently did not practice castration. This time around it turns out that Dinah was never raped (it was a passionate love affair), and the Shechemites were not massacred: Mitchell likes to erase such crude features.

Elsewhere, Mitchell idealizes the personages of both Potiphar and the Pharaoh and quips that Joseph's Egyptian wife, Asenath (Gen.41.45), was "as Gentile as they come," when the Bible merely says that she was the daughter of a priest, and turns her into a model of tender perfection (even as he exalts another shiksa, the pregnant widow Tamar, for risking death by not directly accusing Judah, the father of her twin boys, Perez and Zerah). Joseph's marriage is from first to last so close to perfection that it strains credulity. But that's all part of life in a lovely, imagined exotic land that is eons away from the genocidal Egypt of Exodus 1.8 and the evil Pharaoh "who did not know Joseph."

Mitchell's Joseph is not just "a goodly person and well favored" (Gen. 39.6), but dazzlingly handsome, charming, and omnicompetent. No wonder Potiphar's (unnamed) wife went crazy over him. But Joseph conquers the false accusation against him and shoots up the ladder of power until he's not just the viceroy, but for most practical purposes the ruler of Egypt. It's the ultimate career coup, parallel in part to the success of

Mordecai in the court of Ahasuerus, and Daniel (the supreme dream-interpreter) in the courts of Nebuchadnezzar, Belshazzar, and Darius.

Joseph's planning and providing for the seven lean years of famine saved both the Egyptian people and his own family who came to Egypt as refugees. But there was a price for all this: the virtual enslavement of the Egyptian population to the Pharaoh. All that carefully gathered grain from the fat years had to be bought from government storehouses (why not distribute it as welfare?). The payments were first in cash (but Mitchell's Joseph overcharges the rich and undercharges the poor), then, when the money ran out, in livestock, and finally in land. As Genesis 47.20-21 (RSV) bluntly puts it:

> And Joseph bought all the land of Egypt for Pharaoh; for all the Egyptians sold their fields, because the famine was severe upon them. The land became Pharaoh's; and as for the people, he made slaves of them, from one end of Egypt to the other.

Meanwhile, he had already settled his extended family "in the best of the land, in the land of Rameses" (Gen. 47.11). How clean, then, were Joseph's political hands? And, in view of this, could the "hard bondage" inflicted by the hostile Pharaoh on the children of Israel in Exodus be a karmic payback for the sufferings of the Egyptian masses inflicted by the earlier Pharaoh under Joseph's direction?

But all this comes as a postlude after the grand climactic scene of the reunion between Joseph and his brothers, justly celebrated for its tenderness and humanity. Still, Joseph's various tricks—imprisoning the brothers for three days, placing money in the brothers' sacks (which looked like a set-up) and the silver cup in Benjamin's sack (after demanding that Benjamin leave the anguished Jacob and come to Egypt), putting off his tear-drenched self-revelation and his brothers' amazed *anagnorisis*—while creating a maximum dramatic effect (a bit like the Pharaoh's persistent refusal to let the children of Israel go despite the accumulating plagues)—all this introduces a tense element of what might be considered cruelty into the whole adventure.

Why the three trips before everyone is reunited? In Gen. 42.37 Reuben guarantees poor Jacob that he will bring back Benjamin alive, adding "Slay my two sons, if I bring him not to thee" (Gen. 42.37). That ugly and unlikely touch seems to have been too brutal for Mitchell, so he omits it altogether.

But since long before that, once Joseph had acquired a position of power and confidence, first with Potiphar and then the Pharaoh, why couldn't he at least have sent a message to Jacob, Benjamin, and the rest that all was well with him? Mitchell argues somewhat convolutedly that there was no way Jacob was going to leave Canaan (nor could Joseph, once attached to Pharaoh's service, leave Egypt); and finally, Joseph couldn't assure the safety of his brothers' traveling to Egypt. But even so, wouldn't a letter full of convincing details have brought hope to the mourning family during his long absence? He could have omitted the shameful parts about the kidnapping and substituted some plausible fiction to spare his brothers' position with his father. Instead, he let something like two decades pass by in complete silence.

Having carefully studied his brothers (who can't recognize the harsh Egyptian-speaking official as their kin), Joseph knows that they have already repented their crime; and so, in a way there is no need for forgiveness, noble and heartbreakingly sincere as it is. Then, at the culminating point, Joseph announces the moral of the story:

> "God sent me ahead of you to save lives," he said. Since they all believed in God's power to do whatever He wants—at least Joseph presumed that they did, being sons of his father—they might be able to realize that there are no accidents in the world. Everything happens according to God's will, Everything that happens, whether apparently good or apparently bad, is meant to happen, precisely because it did happen; though the future has infinite possibilities, the past has only one.

Thus far Mitchell's buoyant theology. The near-murder and selling of Joseph into slavery was a *felix culpa*, because it brought down such lavish blessings on the perpetrator, their victim, and the family members who loved him. There are a number of Christian echoes in Mitchell's retelling; but at one point he explicitly backs off from likening Joseph's thinking to Jesus': Stunned by the sight of Joseph come alive again, Jacob wonders if this could be some kind of resurrection. But no, he decides, "life becomes death, death doesn't become life." Jesus may have said (Jn. 12.24) that a grain of wheat has to die to bring forth new, fruitful life. "Ah," replies Jacob-Mitchell, "the metaphor is false. The seed hadn't been dead. It had just been dormant: life in a slower form."

Or is this a Jewish version of the tragic Greek belief that wisdom comes through suffering (even as Judah "wised up" after he almost condemned Tamar to death—by burning!—for getting pregnant out of wedlock). All of history (the Bible in a nutshell) is salvation history; and Mitchell bears eloquent witness to this. It's no surprise that, after having written so sympathetically about all sorts of religion, he should, in his conclusion, echo the final words of Georges Bernanos' *Diary of a Country Priest*: "Everything, even the most painful experience, turns out to be pure grace" (*"Tout est grâce"*), a line that might be hard to square with the Egyptian experience of the Exodus; but that's an argument for another day.

Then again his brothers' sin, once Joseph was a free man on the road to glory in Egypt, brought him such spectacular rewards that he might ultimately have looked back on the whole thing with a kind of complacent irony.

His brothers were still living as pastoral nobodies; he was an international mover-and-shaker. Let bygones be bygones, with a bit of *Schadenfreude*? As the son of Jacob's adored Rachel, Joseph always was his father's favorite (along with Benjamin); and now he had pulled off a sensational rescue of the whole disgraceful lot of them. And then too time sometimes does indeed heal all wounds. Why hold a grudge forever?

But Mitchell's Joseph wouldn't stoop to such lowly thinking. After all, he too has had a saving purgative experience in the ditch, his youthful arrogance and unabashed superiority have turned into a permanent instinctive humility; so he wouldn't dream of settling scores. One wonders if Mitchell's readers will be soft-hearted enough to wholly accept his hero's conclusion, as he looks back on his past, that "There was nothing in it that he could call evil —not the pit, not the prison [but what about the poor baker, who was hanged by Pharaoh?—PH], not slander, famine, destruction, death," because it had all led to such a rapturous denouement.

For modern scriptural scholars, the story of Joseph is plainly an edifying fiction. (There are traces of the Egyptian "Tale of Two Brothers" in the attempted seduction by Potiphar's wife, although John L. McKenzie says, "The Egyptian coloring and background is mostly authentic.") Mitchell adds to the edification by expanding on and delving into the Bible's typically hinted-at psychological depths. As Erich Auerbach pointed out in *Mimesis* (1946), Genesis 22 never tells us what was going on in the minds of Abraham and Isaac on their dreadful three-day journey to Mount Moriah for the Aqedah— but it invites us to probe into what must have been their (especially Abraham's) unspeakable terrors.

Similarly, Mitchell takes the spare narrative of Genesis 37-45 and creates a believable persona of extraordinary sensitivity and selflessness:

> Joseph's confidence was not in himself–or rather, it was not in any self that he could identify. It was in what remained when he stepped aside from the self he knew as Joseph. In that state of inner alertness, he became the listener, with no intentions, no preoccupations, no opinions to defend. The still, small voice [cf. 1 Kings 19.12] that arose inside him was the voice of God, but it was also the voice of reason, stripped of the ordinary selfish distortions that desire and aversion impose.

This mystical, Zen-ish Joseph, "couldn't help hearing the word *misfortune* as a failure of insight. A misfortune is a blessing that has not yet been recognized." So, he is less the epitome of virtue or heroic holy man than a sort of kindly magician who works miracles by spontaneous cooperation with a indefinable, omnipotent cosmic force called God. It's an engaging fantasy, and Mitchell lets it play out beautifully.

—*Peter Heinegg*

CROSSCURRENTS
CONTRIBUTORS

Samuel B. Davis is the Lead Co-Editor Sam Davis will proof his own article as well as the Interview with Dr. Orsi. As a student in both the UNC Charlotte Religious Studies Graduate Department and Women's and Gender Studies program, Sam is currently completing a master's thesis on how the Vatican's handling of sexual abuse by priests is represented and depicted by Catholic news media. Last year, Sam helped organize a graduate conference titled, "Sex and Religion," sponsored by both departments to which he belongs. That conference was held at UNC Charlotte's Center City Campus in the spring of 2019 and was a primary inspiration and source of material for this journal issue. Sam lives in Charlotte, NC with his beautiful, supportive, and talented partner Amanda and their two cats.

sdavi230@uncc.edu

Delaney James is a first-year law student at Wake Forest University School of Law. She obtained her bachelor's degree in political science with minors in both religious studies and communications from Elon University.

delaney.k.james@gmail.com

Peter Heinegg was born in Brooklyn, spent seven years in Jesuit seminaries, and received a B.A. in English from Fordham University and a Ph.D. in Comparative Literature from Harvard University. He has taught at Harvard, Queens College, C.U.N.Y and at Union College in Schenectady, where he is a professor of English and Comparative Literature. He is the author of numerous translations of books on religion and theology, of book reviews, and volumes of collected essays on religion and contemporary culture. He has contributed to the Christianity section of the Norton Anthology of World Religion. His special interests include the Bible, anti-Semitism, and the history of belief and unbelief in nineteenth-century Europe.

peterheinegg@hotmail.com

Morgan van Kesteren is a student at Colgate University, majoring in Classical Studies, minoring in Psychology, and following the pre-med track. Studying Latin and Greek languages and culture, Morgan examines classical literature while focusing on patterns that reflect the contemporary world. While translating the *Aeneid* during a Latin class, Morgan remarked on the parallels between the homoerotic relations of Nisus and Euryalus and Achilles and Pallas in the *Iliad*. Fascinated with the different types of love presented in ancient epic, Morgan examined Plato's *Symposium* as a lens for discerning ancient cultural beliefs about love. Morgan presented this paper at the UNCC Sex and Religion Conference in the spring of 2019.

mvankesteren@colgate.edu

Jessi Knippel is an academic, writer, and artist who lives in the promised land of Southern California with her partner and tiny human. She is currently working on an intersectional Ph.D. at Claremont Graduate School in gender, religion, and media. A muralist at heart she pieces together projects, events, thoughts, and people in her work and non-work life. You can see her various works on Instagram—@seattlerainartist; on Twitter—@jessiknippel; and at www.jessiknippel.com.

Jessica.knippel@cgu.edu
seattlerainartist@gmail.com

Caroline Norma lectures in the Master of Translation and Interpreting degree at RMIT University in Melbourne, Australia. She researches histories of military and civilian prostitution systems in Asia and the Pacific from a feminist abolitionist perspective. She is involved in a range of abolitionist organizations in Australia and Japan, including the Tokyo-based People Against Pornography and Sexual Violence (PAPS).

caroline.norma@rmit.edu.au

Ashley Starr-Morris is an American scholar, writer, and activist living in Southern California with her circus of one amazing spouse, a newly added tiny human, and two big furball pups. She is currently earning her Ph.D. in Women and Religion at Claremont Graduate University, doing the work her soul must have. Her research is inspired by the many women in her own life who encouraged her to liberate her voice and make known the silenced voices of others.

ashley.starr-morris@cgu.edu

Pamela D. Winfield is Associate Professor of Religious Studies at Elon University, NC. Her first book, Icons and Iconoclasm in Japanese Buddhism: Kūkai and Dōgen on the Art of Enlightenment (Oxford University Press, 2013) won the Association of Asian Studies – Southeast Conference Book Prize in 2015. Her second book is a co-edited volume with Steven Heine entitled Zen and Material Culture (Oxford University Press, 2017). Her numerous articles and book chapters have appeared in The Japanese Journal of Religious Studies, Material Religion: The Journal of Objects, Art and Belief, Religion Compass, Religious Studies Review, and the Southeast Review of Asian Studies, as well as in publications by Oxford University Press, Columbia University Press, Brill, and Routledge.

pwinfield@elon.edu

www.ingramcontent.com/pod-product-compliance
Lightning Source LLC
Chambersburg PA
CBHW040300170426
43193CB00020B/2954